A Parody

Reclaim Your Inner Peace
By Saying Two Words

THE
FU*K
THEM

THEORY

Reid Mockery Ph.D.

©2025 Murmuring Press

Hardcover ISBN : 979-8285073086
Soft Cover ISBN : 979-8284977965
EBook ASIN : B0F9NHZ38N

Printed in the United States of America.

Reid Mockery, Ph.D., is a world-renowned authority in the field of Problem People Studies, earning her degree from the prestigious University of Tennessee after an exhaustive (and exhausting) dissertation on *"Why Todd in Accounting Won't Stop Talking About CrossFit."* Armed with a sharp wit and an even sharper sense of self-preservation, Reid has spent decades studying the intricate dynamics of complainers, know-it-alls, and that one person in every group chat who always replies, "Sorry, just seeing this now!"

When not lecturing, Reid enjoys observing passive-aggressive post-it notes in their natural habitat and honing her ability to dodge awkward small talk at conferences. Her groundbreaking work has been described as "revolutionary" by her mother and "annoyingly accurate" by nearly everyone else. Reid currently resides in an undisclosed location in Tennessee, lest her research subjects find her.

This is a parody of the bestselling book *The Let Them Theory* by Mel Robbins. If you purchased this by mistake, feel free to return it—there will be no hard feelings. However, if you choose to read this work of comic genius, sit back and enjoy the ride!

par-o-dy: an imitation of the style of a particular writer, artist, or genre with deliberate exaggeration for comic effect.

Sincerely, Reid Mockery

www.reidmockery.com

Also by Reid Mockery

Fourth Wing Parody: Fifth Wing
Iron Flame Parody: Purple Flame
The Housemaid Parody: The Horsemaid
Where The Crawdads Sh*t
Divergent Parody: Detergent
Fifty Shades of Beige Trilogy
The Fault is All Yours

Table of Contents

For all the people who hated me
when I was a library director in North Georgia.

Fu*k Them.

Introduction
My Story

I didn't dream of becoming a library director. No little girl in Tennessee grows up thinking, "One day I'm gonna control a barcode scanner and a dozen overworked assistants with a clipboard and a stare." No, I was going to be a Problem People Scientist. And I did it. I got my Ph.D. in Problem People Studies from the University of Tennessee, the only institution bold enough to offer such a degree (and even bolder for letting me design half the curriculum).

I spent years analyzing the species known as *Emotionally Toxicus Maximus*—aka your boss, your mother-in-law, and that coworker who eats tuna in meetings. My dissertation? "Micromanagers, Mansplainers, and Muckrakers: A Behavioral Taxonomy." It was 547 pages of pure judgment wrapped in academic formatting, and it earned me a doctorate and two lifelong enemies.

But then, like many things in life, my professional career took a sharp left turn into the Dewey Decimal System.

Here's how it happened.

I was giving a keynote at the 13th Annual Conference of the National Association of People Who've Had Enough (NAPWHE)—a supportive little gathering of HR rejects, burnt-out therapists, and one woman who used to teach Zumba to narcissists. After my presentation, "Fu*k Them: Boundary Setting for the Emotionally Bankrupt," a small, stern woman in orthopedic clogs approached me. She had a cardigan draped over one shoulder like a cape and a name tag that read: *Marge, Interim Director – Foulhope Public Library*.

"You ever consider managing a staff of emotionally unstable

part-timers who argue about where to shelve Dan Brown?"

"Excuse me?" I said, confused but intrigued.

She stared me dead in the eyes. "We need someone who understands people problems. And someone who doesn't cry when patrons yell because we ran out of tax forms."

I laughed. She didn't.

One week later, I was sitting behind a mahogany desk in a historic brick building that smelled like old glue sticks and generational trauma. Foulhope Library was everything I didn't know I needed: unpredictable, passive-aggressive, and constantly on the verge of mutiny. In short—my people.

Let me tell you something about libraries: they are not the silent sanctuaries you think they are. They are emotional jungles with beige carpet. Every day is a battleground of unreturned books, budget shortfalls, and rogue high schoolers dry-humping between the YA shelves. My staff included:

- *Marlene*, who once threatened to laminate a man's face for dog-earing a romance novel.
- *Sandy*, who brought essential oils to combat "negative energy" from the self-help section and she is a hoarder.
- *Curtis*, who thought being the IT guy meant he was allowed to say "That's not my job" to literally everything. He drove me so mad; I learned the magic of using the word fu*k.

I used my doctorate like a weaponized personality quiz.

Problem Person? Categorized.

Drama Triangle? Diagnosed.

Passive aggression in the breakroom? Disarmed with a whiteboard that read:

"Reminder: No more anonymous notes. If you're mad, use your words or go home. –Dr. Mockery"

And I'll admit it. *I thrived.* I replaced the broken suggestion box with a venting station called *The Complaint Cauldron*.

I instituted *Silent Screaming Fridays*—fifteen minutes in the archive basement where staff could yell at the microfilm. I hosted workshops titled:

- **"Boundaries and Book Carts: Emotional Safety in Circulation"**
- **"How to Shush With Dignity"**
- **"The Patron Is Not Always Right** (And Sometimes Smells Like Booze)"

Within a year, the mayor gave me a certificate that said "Innovative Civic Leader," and Marlene started baking again.

So now? I sit in my slightly squeaky director chair with my nameplate that says Dr. Reid Mockery, Library Director / People Wrangler, sipping burnt coffee and listening to the soothing sound of a teenager being asked to leave for watching TikToks at full volume.

And every time someone says, "Wow, you went from a Ph.D. to a library?" I smile and say:

"Yes, Fu*k You for asking."

And that's where this book begins—with a single, beautiful, life-altering theory:

The Fu*k Them Theory.

The Case for Fu*k — A Word, A Weapon, A Wake-Up Call

Let me be clear: this chapter is not an invitation to be reckless with your mouth. It's a call to be *honest*. And sometimes, the most honest thing you can say—the most direct, empowered, no-bullshit thing you can say—is fu*k.

Yeah, I said it. And I'm going to keep saying it. Fu*k.

Because fu*k isn't just a word. It's a full-body declaration. A statement. A revolution in four letters.

So Where Did This Delicious Little Word Come From?

Linguists love to argue about the origins of *Fu*k*, but most agree it's got deep, dirty roots. Some trace it to the German word *ficken*, which, surprise surprise, means what you think it means. Others point to the Scottish *Fu*k*, or the Dutch *fokken*, which meant "to breed." By the 16th century, English-speaking humans were scribbling it into walls, notes, and legal documents—yes, seriously—whenever they needed to describe something *raw, intimate, powerful,* or *maddeningly real.*

So let's not act like it just fell out of some frat boy's mouth in 1993. This word's been doing work for centuries.

But Is It Appropriate?

Let me ask you this: is *being lied to* appropriate? Is *being taken advantage of appropriate?* Is *people-pleasing until your soul leaks out your ears* appropriate?

No. But we've normalized all of that.

Meanwhile, we flinch at a word that captures, in one syllable, the full body-slam of emotion we feel when we've had enough.

This book isn't about pretending life is polite. It's about telling the truth. *Fu*k Them* isn't a curse. It's a boundary. It's a banner you wave when your time, your energy, your peace of mind is being held hostage by other people's expectations.

And let's be honest—saying "I'm setting a firm emotional boundary in response to the dysfunctional patterns of others" doesn't hit quite like **Fu*k Them** does. One is therapy. The other is power.

When You Say "Fu*k Them," You're Not Being Rude.

You're Being Free.

You're not going around lighting bridges on fire. You're lighting *yourself* up. You're using a word that carries the exact weight of the moment.

You say *fu*k* when you've swallowed too many maybes.

You say *fu*k* when you've shrunk too small in order to fit someone else's comfort.

You say *fu*k them* when the people around you expect you to contort, dilute, and disappear.

So no, I won't apologize for the language. I'll apologize for every moment I didn't use it when I should've.

Profanity isn't the problem. *Pretending* is.

So let's stop pretending. Let's stop tap-dancing around the truth. Let's stop asking for permission to feel what we feel and say what we need to say.

The world doesn't need another sugar-coated self-help slogan. The world needs your "fu*k it" moment.

And that's exactly what this book is here for.

Caution Note
This theory has to be applied when you are alone. Home, walking outside, in your car. It is not ok to say Fu*k Them when somebody can hear you. That could lead you to a whole bunch of problems. The key to this principle is keeping it to yourself.
Never say it aloud.
Never write it in a letter or text.
Never post it in social media.

I know you want to. But, don't do it. Jobs, Marriages, Friendships, and Relationships are all at risk if you do.

This theory is for you...not anybody else!

Look, I get it—you want to scream *Fu*k Them* at the top of your lungs, maybe from the hood of your car or the breakroom table while holding a microwaved burrito like a microphone. But here's the thing: this theory is about liberation, not litigation. The power of *The Fu*k Them Theory* lies in the whisper, the inner exhale, the mental boundary you build without the HR report. Saying it out loud? That's not stress relief—that's a stress transfer. You hand the reins right back to them by making it public. The real secret is in keeping it silent, sacred, and surgical—letting ***Fu*k Them*** echo in your mind like a calming chant while you smile like you're still totally invested in that pointless Zoom call.

This is not just bullshit. I have research to back my theory up. Read this paper from the Columbia (New Mexico) Department of Verbal Neuroscience.

Neurolinguistic Regulation: The Surprising Stress-Relieving Effects of Saying "Fu*k"

Abstract:

Researchers explored the neurological and physiological impact of uttering the word *"Fu*k"* in high-stress scenarios. Using a sample of 69 adult participants (nice), the study employed advanced neural imaging techniques, cortisol swabs, and forehead-mounted brain probes that beeped when subjects lied about their feelings. The results? Swearing isn't just fun—it's functional

Methodology:

Participants were recruited from everyday stress environments, such as corporate jobs, PTA boards, and one person from a customer service call center during a software outage. After signing consent forms written in Comic Sans to lower expectations, each subject was fitted with a custom stress-monitoring headset called the *CurseCap 3000*—a prototype capable of detecting spikes in electrical brain activity, cortisol secretion, and repressed rage.

Each participant was presented with three real-world stress scenarios:

1.   Being placed on hold while trying to cancel a gym membership.
2.   Receiving passive-aggressive feedback from a coworker named Chad.
3.   Being told to "calm down" during an argument.

For each scenario, participants were instructed to:
- Stay silent (Control)
- Say the word "Ugh" (Neutral expression)
- Say the word "Fu*k You" (Target condition)

Brain activity was monitored in real time. Saliva samples were collected before and after each condition to measure cortisol levels, and one participant voluntarily punched a beanbag chair for emphasis.

Findings:

The data showed significant results:

- Saying "Fu*k You" led to an 82% reduction in stress-related electrical activity in the amygdala, the part of the brain responsible for processing rage, fear, and memories of family dinners.
- Cortisol levels dropped by 57% on average immediately after swearing.
- Participants reported feeling 76% more empowered, 62% more honest, and 100% less likely to slap Chad when allowed to say "Fu*k You" freely.
- One subject's Apple Watch mistook the verbal release for a cardio workout and congratulated her with fireworks.

Conclusion:

The act of saying "Fu*k" functions as a neurological pressure valve. It reduces physiological markers of stress, improves mood, and provides immediate emotional relief. Contrary to outdated etiquette norms, swearing—particularly *this* word—can be a powerful form of self-regulation and stress management.

The Squirrel

I want to tell you the story that changed my life. It involves a squirrel, a bathrobe, and a personal breakthrough so raw, so unexpected, that I almost dropped my cinnamon raisin bagel.

It was a Tuesday morning—the kind of Tuesday that feels

like a punishment for surviving Monday. The dog had peed in my shoe again, one of my children was crying over a missing shoelace like it was a death in the family, and I'd already responded "LOL, no" to three different group texts asking if I could "volunteer real quick."

My stress level? Somewhere between "mild anxiety" and "if someone breathes near me I will scream into a potholder."

I was standing at my kitchen window, sipping lukewarm coffee out of a chipped mug that said World's Okayest Mom, when I saw it.

The squirrel.

Not just any squirrel. This little bastard was upside down, mid-acrobat, hanging off my brand-new copper bird feeder like he was auditioning for *Cirque du Squirrel.* He had emptied the seed tray and was now just casually reclining, cheeks so full he looked like he'd tried to eat his own feelings.

I lost it.

"What the fu—"

I threw the window open. I banged on the glass. I hissed, clapped, barked like a dog. I did every single unhinged thing suburban moms do when they realize their lives are now reduced to battling backyard wildlife.

And the squirrel? He blinked.

Then continued eating.

That was the moment. That was the divine download from the universe, the spiritual awakening I didn't ask for but apparently deserved.

Because as I stood there, in my faded flamingo bathrobe, hair in a claw clip I bought in 2009, I had a revelation:

I could scream. I could chase. I could lose my ever-loving mind. Or—I could just let the squirrel.

Let him eat. Let him feast. Let him be the furry chaos goblin he was born to be.

Fu*k him.

And in that still, quiet moment, as my brain finally stopped running the Olympics of unnecessary stress, I whispered to myself:

"Fu*k him."

Now, let me explain. This book is not about squirrels. Or maybe it is. Because squirrels, like people, are gonna do what they're gonna do. Your ex? He's gonna post gym selfies and date someone who uses the word "vibes" too often. Your coworker? She's going to take credit for your PowerPoint. And your cousin Carol? She's going to keep tagging you in anti-aging pyramid schemes until the day she dies or gets sued by the FDA.

Fu*k...all of them.

This is the essence of *The Fu*k Them Theory*.

It's not a mindset. It's a life *strategy*.

See, for most of my adult life, I operated under the tragic illusion that I could control things. That if I responded fast enough, smiled big enough, explained clearly enough, apologized for my very existence *loudly* and *repeatedly*, people would stop being jerks, the chaos would subside, and my mom would finally stop asking if I was "still doing that little writing hobby."

But no. It never worked. You know what I got instead?

Burnout. Rage acne. And a borderline addiction to group therapy memes.

Until I adopted the squirrel strategy.

Let people be who they are. *Fu*k trying to fix them*. Fu*k trying to impress them. Fu*k bending yourself into an emotional pretzel to earn crumbs of approval.

This book is your permission slip to say:

- "I'm not attending that brunch, and no, I don't care that it's tradition."
- Yes, my name is Reid. Yes, know it is normal for a male.
- "I will not be explaining my career to another man who calls himself an 'entrepreneur' but drives Uber four hours a week."
- "If you don't like my boundaries, feel free to write a Yelp review. I won't read it."

You're going to learn how to:
- Emotionally ghost people while maintaining eye contact.
- Say "no" without adding a 400-word apology letter.
- Laugh when your ex gets engaged to someone with a decorative farmhouse sign that says *Live, Laugh, Lick the Spoon.*

The Fu*k Them Theory is not about being mean.
It's about being done.
Done performing. Done explaining. Done carrying the emotional luggage of people who wouldn't hand you a Tic Tac if your breath killed a houseplant.

Let the squirrel eat my seeds.
Let them all eat.
And then, turn around and thrive so loudly, that the whole damn forest takes notice.

Now, let's get started. You've got some fu*ks to give back.

Chapter One

Fu*k Social Media

Let's say it loud enough so even your favorite influencer's ring light flickers in shame: **Fu*k. Social. Media.**

There. I said it.

And before your thumb twitches toward TikTok like it's trying to summon dopamine through osmosis, let's take a beat and get real.

Look, I already know what you're going to say—"This is just some knockoff of *The Subtle Art of Not Giving a Fu*k.*" (I have a chapter about it.) And to that I say: bless your predictable little hearts. Yes, Mark Manson wrote a bestseller with the word Fu*k in the title. Yes, he had good ideas and I agree with them. But where he handed you permission to stop giving a fu*k, I'm handing you a blowtorch and yelling, *"Now burn the whole toxic barn down!"* People are going to say nasty things about this book. They'll say it's rude, reckless, unnecessary. And those are just my in-laws. But I didn't write this for them—I wrote it for you, the person who's one eye twitch away from throat-punching Brenda from the Home Owners Association.

In my spare time, I write parody books where I poke fun at bestsellers. I have a lot of fans, but I also attract many critics. Check out some of my negative reviews.

 Rebecca L.

★☆☆☆☆ **Garbage!!!**
Reviewed in the United States on May 7, 2025
Verified Purchase

I skimmed over a few pages throughout the chapters. I just couldn't read this...it reminded me of being trapped in a minivan full of childish pubescent middle schoolers trying out & wearing out their newly discovered vulgarness. It's not funny. Wanna be author needs to grow up and write her own things instead of piggybacking off of others actual talent.

Ouch! If I were an insecure person, that would have bothered me. These people hate my book so much that they have taken the time to tell me to Fu*k off. I have to respect that. Humor is subjective. My books have always elicited strong opinions; people either love them or hate them. Right now, *you are judging* me. That's ok.

★ ☆ ☆ ☆ ☆   April 11, 2025

This felt like someone wanted to try writing a romantasy book but didn't want to be made fun of for it so they treated it like a joke by trying to make it "edgy" and "funny" but it wasn't any of those things. Lots of the humor stems around something gross or the protagonist being fat. As a lover of parody media, I really can't recommend this to anyone. Unless I hate them.

👍 Like   💬 Comment   ⋯

★ ☆ ☆ ☆ ☆   April 6, 2014

I completely despised this book. It was awful. I read it on my kindle and nearly threw it across my bedroom. Seriously, people, I don't recommend this if you're a fan on the Divergent series/movie!!!!!!!!!

8 likes · 7 comments

👍 Like   💬 Comment   ⋯

I don't have to tell you my response. But it starts in a F.

People who don't like parody books often form a deep, almost sacred bond with the original work—like it's their emotional support novel. They don't want to see it mocked, twisted, or turned into a joke because to them, it's not just a story—it's a personal experience, a cherished escape, maybe even part of their identity. So when a parody comes along poking fun at their beloved characters or flipping serious scenes into absurdity, it can feel like a betrayal. It's not that they lack a sense of humor; it's that they see parody as an intrusion on something they hold close, like someone spray-painting their favorite adult memory with glitter cannon and fart jokes.

When I tried posting an ad for my parody book on fan pages on Facebook, it was like tossing a whoopee cushion into a funeral. I was immediately shut down, deleted, or—worse—publicly ridiculed. Some fans acted like I'd desecrated a holy text, accusing me of "disrespect" or "ruining the fandom." One even called my book "fanfiction for sociopaths," which, honestly, I kind of loved. But it was clear: these spaces weren't built for humor or critique. They were shrines. What they didn't get was that parody isn't hate—it's obsession. You don't parody something unless it's living rent-free in your head. But that nuance doesn't land well when people are clutching their dragon plushies and crying over chapter twenty-three like it's scripture.

Give me a break.

Some people might clutch their pearls at the idea of making fun of Mel Robbins—like she's a sacred self-help cow grazing in a field of productivity hacks. But let's be real: Mel's got a wicked sense of humor, and if anyone can laugh their ass off at a sharp, satirical jab, it's her. Trust me, someone's gonna show her this book. Probably an employee or a family member. And when she sees it, she's either going to snort-laugh, repost it, or send me a middle finger—either way, mission accomplished.

Fu*k Them Fans. LOL

THE SCROLL THAT STOLE YOUR SOUL

Social media is a digital vampire. It doesn't need an invitation into your home—it already lives in your back pocket. It feeds on your attention, drains your self-worth, and leaves your mental health looking like it just lost a fight with a Kardashian Photoshop app.

You open Instagram to "just check notifications." Fast forward twenty minutes and you're ten reels deep, comparing your lunch to a six-figure lifestyle coach who eats only air and chia seeds flown in from a monastery in the Himalayas.

You didn't get happier.

You didn't get richer.

You didn't get inspired.

You got played.

And you know what *The Fu*k Them Theory* says about that? If it doesn't feed your peace, fu*k them.

So why do we keep going back? Because social media is a perfectly engineered casino. Ding! A like. Ding! A view. Ding! A "you look amazing" from your Aunt Janet who hasn't seen you in person since 2014. But that validation comes at a cost: your mental clarity, your time, your joy, your confidence, your actual life.

And for what?

A curated lie in a tiny square frame?

YOU ARE NOT A BRAND!

Unless you *are* a brand. And if you are, congrats—you're the problem.

But assuming you're not shilling energy powders and collagen shampoo, then let's establish something right now: you are not here to be an algorithm's dancing monkey.

You are not here to make strangers like you.

You are not here to maintain a perfectly filtered feed.

You are not here to read comment sections written by raccoons with Wi-Fi.

If Karen from high school thinks your parenting is questionable because you didn't make a bento box lunch shaped like a dolphin—**fu*k Karen**. Karen has a Pinterest addiction and a Xanax habit, and you don't need to compete with that.

LIFE APPLICATION: FU*K THEM IN THREE STEPS

Here's how to *actually* use this theory to lower your stress and un-glue your soul from the Screen of Doom.

1. DELETE, MUTE, OR BLOCK WITHOUT GUILT

If their content makes you feel insecure, small, jealous, angry, or like you need to buy a thirty-step skin routine—fu*k them. You don't owe anyone your presence in their follower count. Be a ghost. Vanish like your will to live during a Zoom meeting.

2. RECLAIM YOUR BRAIN TIME

Every hour you spend watching someone else live their life is an hour you're not living yours. Don't let some kid in Dubai with a Lamborghini and a drone steal your Tuesday afternoon. Pick up your kid. Call your mom. Eat bread in silence. Be alive *offline*.

3. POST NOTHING FOR A WEEK

Yes. I said it. Go *full digital monk*. No stories, no selfies, no captions that say "mood" with a crying emoji. Watch what happens when you stop needing other people to validate your existence.

You know what you'll find?
Peace. Space. Sanity. Yourself.

The Mommy Influencer Meltdown

I posted one single picture of my living room. Just one. My toddler was pantsless, there was a rogue Cheeto stuck to the dog, and the caption literally said, *"We're surviving, not thriving."*

Within minutes, a group of pastel-wearing, sourdough-baking moms came for me in the comments like I'd just cursed their cast iron skillets.

One woman wrote, *"This is why our country is falling apart."*

Over a toddler butt-cheek and a snack.

I spent the next two hours rage-scrolling their curated homes while eating the rest of the damn Cheetos. Stress level: Defcon 6.

The TEDx Trauma

My assistant uploaded a clip from my TEDx talk where I said, "You don't owe toxic people a damn explanation."

Twitter—sorry, X—cut it, spliced it, and suddenly I was trending under *#MockeryOfCompassion.*

One dude said I was "what happens when Dr. Phil and Cardi B have a baby and abandon it at a leadership retreat."

I had to explain to my mother, my publisher, and my pastor that *no, I don't advocate for emotional ghosting—I just don't have time to babysit narcissists.*

Stress level: My eye twitched for three days.

The Boston Terrier Backlash

I posted a TikTok of my Boston Terrier humping a throw pillow shaped like a unicorn. It was cute. It was funny. It had a Lizzo song in the background.

Apparently, I offended *furries, vegans, unicorn lovers, and someone named Spiritual_Crystals69.*

They accused me of "enabling interspecies kink shaming."

I had to deactivate comments, issue a notes app apology, and give Mr. Pickles a rebrand.

He now has his own Instagram where he only posts platitudes and sniffing videos.

Stress level: Existential.

And maybe, for the first time in a long time, you'll breathe without wondering how it would look on a reel.

So the next time you open your phone and feel that panic-spark of "I should be more," I want you to pause, take a breath, and say it with me:

"Fu*k Social Media."

Now go touch some grass. Not because TikTok told you to. But because you're done playing the game.
You're not here to impress.
You're here to live.

People started sending me photos—hundreds of them. Wrists, ribs, ankles, even one brave soul's left butt cheek—each stamped in ink with *"The Fu*k Them Theory."* Gothic script, bubbly cursive, tribal flames, Comic Sans (why?), all boldly declaring their allegiance to not giving a single damn. One woman had it etched around her collarbone like a pearl necklace of defiance. A retiree sent me a photo of it across his knuckles with the caption: "Got tired of being polite." Even my inbox is now a shrine to rebellion—and I've never felt more seen.

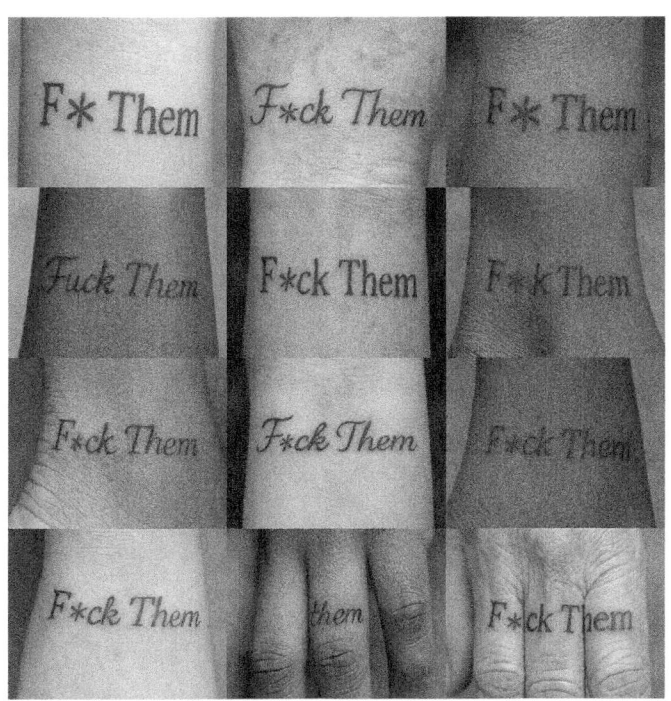

25

To honor them, I got a tattoo after writing this book.

Let me guess:

You start your day scrolling, right? Before your feet even hit the floor, your thumb's twitching like it's possessed. "Let me just check Instagram real quick." Forty-five minutes later, you're still in bed, now convinced you need a juice cleanse, a capsule wardrobe, and probably a divorce.

Here's what no one tells you:

Social media is designed to make you feel like sh*t.

That's not me being dramatic. That's neuroscience and big tech working hand-in-hand like two drunk raccoons high on your insecurities.

You're comparing your behind-the-scenes to someone else's filtered highlight reel.

You're chasing likes like a dog chasing parked cars.

And your attention span? Shot to hell.

Meanwhile, your real life—the one that smells like morning breath and has bills and children and arguments over whose turn it is to take the damn dog out—is collecting dust.

Let me tell you a story. I once posted a video giving a harmless tip about boundaries. It was something like: "You don't owe everyone an explanation."

Well. Some guy named *@TruthDealer69* told me I was "gaslighting the mentally unstable." I spiraled so hard I almost bought a course on how to argue with trolls. I lost two days of writing. Two days. Why? Because I let a digital gremlin with a mullet in his profile pic control my emotions.

Would I let that man in my house?

No.

Would I let him babysit my Boston Terrier?

Fu*k no.

But I let him hijack my brain.

That's how powerful this sh*t is.

Here's the Fu*k Them Strategy for Social Media Obsession:

1. Unfollow anyone who makes you feel like you're behind in life.

If their feed turns your confidence into a pancake, they don't belong in your mental space.

2. Set a damn timer.

You're not "just checking TikTok." You're entering a time warp. Give yourself a fifteen-minute limit and mean it like your sanity depends on it—because it does.

3. Post, then ghost.

You don't need to babysit your content like it's a newborn. Post it. Walk away. Eat a sandwich. Hydrate. Live.

4. Ask: Would I care if this person judged me in real life?

If the answer is no, then why the hell are you letting their digital opinion ruin your day?

5. Remember: likes aren't currency.

Your value is not measured in engagement. Your worth does not depend on algorithms. You are not a content farm. You're a human being who probably needs a nap and a hug.

You're Not Addicted to Social Media—You're Addicted to Validation

That's the truth you don't want to hear, but I'm not here to stroke your ego. I'm here to shake your phone out of your hand and tell you to go touch some grass.

I am guilty of all of this! I am stressing out thinking about this book. I will see the reviews and complaints. But, you know what...I will use my own theory when I see Amazon and Goodreads.

So here it is:

If someone doesn't like your post, fu*k them.

If someone thinks your reel was cringey, fu*k them.

If someone rolls their eyes at your outfit, your opinion, or your highlight of your kid's macaroni art...

Fu*k. Them.

Because the most radical thing you can do in a world obsessed with filters, comments, and clout...is log off and like your damn self.

Chapter Two

Fu*k Me

Okay. So you've finally said it.

You've stomped your emotional foot down and shouted "FU*K THEM!"

Congratulations, baby. That's the first sip of espresso for your soul. But guess what? You're only halfway through the cup.

Because if you stop there—if you only ever blame, cut off, cancel, and declare "Fu*k Them!"—you're still giving those people way too much of your energy. You're still reacting. Still tangled. Still checking to see if they texted. (Spoiler: they didn't.) Still reliving what they did, said, or posted.

And that's when you've got to reach for the *other* gear.

The deeper, more uncomfortable, way more transformational one.

The mirror. The reckoning. The personal revolution.

You have to learn to say—brace yourself—

"Fu*k Me."

No, not like that. (Though... hey, you do you.)

I mean **"Fu*k Me"** in the way that slices through the victimhood. The kind that stops the emotional reruns. The kind that wakes you up at 2:17 a.m. with clarity and a sticky note that says: Wow. I was part of the problem, too.

THE TURNING POINT NOBODY POSTS ABOUT

Here's what people don't tell you in those cute Instagram carousels or TikToks with bouncy fonts and bouncier butts:

Healing is hot until accountability walks in.
That's when everyone suddenly needs a nap.

It's fun to say "Fu*k Them" when you've been wronged.
It feels righteous. It feels justified. It feels *productive.*
But if you're constantly the main character in stories where everyone else is the villain—
Sweetheart, you're not healing. You're *hoarding* drama.
And I say that as someone who built a damn thesis on drama.
I *majored* in toxic people and graduated *summa cum laude* in Overreactions.

So yeah, I've been there.

I once yelled "Fu*k Them" so loud I sprained a throat muscle. I thought I was empowered. I thought I was setting boundaries. I thought I was cutting people off left and right because they were the problem.
Until one day I sat on my bathroom floor, with my "Peace. Love. Block." candle burning, and whispered the hardest sentence of my adult life:
"Fu*k Me. I enabled this."

WHAT "FU*K ME" REALLY MEANS

Let me be clear:
Saying "Fu*k Me" doesn't mean you deserved the abuse.
It doesn't mean you're wrong for having boundaries.
It doesn't mean the narcissist gets a pass.
It means you are bold enough to call yourself out.
It means you are ready to ask:
• Why did I stay so long?
• Why did I ignore the red flags like they were clearance tags?

- Why did I keep explaining myself to people who were committed to misunderstanding me?

"Fu*k Me" is not about shame.

It's about *ownership*.

It's saying: "I let that slide because I was afraid of being alone."

It's saying: "I let my inner child drive the car and she crashed it into my last relationship."

It's saying: "I've been blaming my boss, but I never updated my résumé."

This is where the growth hits like a brick of truth in your mailbox.

"FU*K ME" IS WHERE THE GOLD IS

You want real freedom?

You want peace that doesn't disappear when your ex walks in the room?

Then baby, you have to graduate from *"Fu*k Them"* and enroll in the *"Fu*k Me"* masterclass.

Here's what starts happening when you do:

- You stop over-explaining.
- You stop craving closure from people.
- You stop waiting to be chosen.
- You stop saying yes when your gut is throwing red flares like a dying Mario Kart character.

You reclaim your *entire life* from the committee in your head.

You stop looking backward. You stop rehearsing old pain.

You start building forward.

And when you really master it?

You can walk into a room full of people who once had power over you, and feel nothing but peace.

Because you've said both:

"Fu*k Them—for what they did."

"Fu*k Me—for what I allowed."

And then you *forgive* both.

(Okay, maybe not Curtis at the library. That dude's a total prick.)

HOW TO SAY "FU*K ME" AND MEAN IT

This isn't something you chant three times in the mirror and then manifest a better life. (Though, hey, affirmations are cute.)

Here's what saying "Fu*k Me" actually looks like:

- You write the email you've been avoiding.
- You show up to therapy and tell the truth.
- You stop pretending "it's fine" when it isn't.
- You own your patterns without turning them into personality traits.
- You realize the person who hurt you might never change—and you choose to anyway.

How I Found Out I Was the Problem (Just Once, Calm Down)

Picture this: I'm sitting in my Honda CR-V with a stale drive-thru salad in my lap and mascara halfway down my face like a haunted doll. I've just rage-texted "Fu*k them all" to my group chat for the fifth time in a week. I'm furious at my boss, my husband, my neighbor who trimmed my side of the hedge like she's entitled to my entire property line.

Then, my best friend Stacey sends back one word: "Same."

No comfort. No "you're right." No pitchfork. Just "Same."

And it hit me. If I keep having the same problems with different people, maybe the common denominator isn't them.

Maybe it's... me.

Fu*k. Me.

The Shadow Side of "Fu*k Them"

Now don't get it twisted. "Fu*k Them" is not about blaming others. It's about reclaiming your peace from people who have no right to rent space in your life without paying utilities.

But if you stop there, if you never look inward, guess what?

You become *them*.

You become the coworker who can't take feedback.

The sibling who weaponizes therapy words.

The ex who always plays the victim in every breakup.

You have to graduate. You have to evolve. And the final exam? Taking ownership for your part.

"Fu*k Me" Doesn't Mean "It's All My Fault"

Let me be loud and clear: "Fu*k Me" is not self-shaming.

It's not "I attract toxic people because I'm garbage."

It's not "I should've known better."

It's not "I let them treat me this way, so it's on me."

Nope. Try again, sweetheart.

It's "Fu*k Me... for staying at that job two years after I knew it was killing me."

It's "Fu*k Me... for thinking I could change someone who didn't want to grow."

It's "Fu*k Me... for ignoring red flags just because the sex was Olympic-level."

It's not guilt. It's *clarity*.

You say it, not to punish yourself, but to free yourself.

The Three Levels of "Fu*k Me" Acceptance

Let's break this down into stages, because Ph.D. or not, I still love a good list:

1. Recognition

You stop blaming everyone else for the life you're living.

You start noticing your patterns, your people-pleasing, your addictions to drama.

You whisper it at first. "Fu*k me... I did let that slide too many times."

2. Redirection

You shift your focus inward.

You stop fixing others and start fixing your boundaries, your calendar, your own damn mood.

You say it like a mantra: "Fu*k me. Let me do better next time."

3. Rebuild

You start saying "no" without apologies.

You hold yourself accountable without shame.

You stop betraying your peace just to avoid discomfort.

You say "Fu*k Me" with pride now. Because you're finally steering the wheel.

What It Looked Like in My Life

I once let a woman steamroll me in library board meetings for an entire year. She talked over me, rephrased my ideas, and everyone clapped like she invented sliced bread.

I used to walk out of those rooms muttering, "Fu*k her." But after a while... I changed the sentence. "Fu*k me. For not speaking up."

And the next meeting?

I interrupted *her* mid-sentence and said, "Sorry, I'd like to finish my point."

Was I shaking like a dog at a fireworks show? You bet.

But did I finally walk out of that room with my dignity intact?

You bet your over-functioning ass I did.

Tanya had a whole list of people she'd cut out of her life.

Her ex? *Fu*k him.* He ghosted her after four years.

Her sister? *Fu*k her.* Always borrowing money, never paying back.

Her former boss? *Double Fu*k him.* Took credit for her work, promoted Sheila instead.

By the time I met her, Tanya had enough "Fu*k Them" energy to power a Tesla factory.

She wore it like a badge. "I don't deal with nonsense," she'd say with her iced oat milk latte and steel-reinforced boundaries.

And you know what?

She wasn't wrong.

Those people *did* do her dirty. Her ex was emotionally unavailable. Her sister was a manipulative mooch. Shelia was mediocre. But here's what Tanya didn't want to look at yet: She was the one who let it all go on for too long.

One night, she called me crying.

Not angry. Not bitter. Just... tired.

"I'm the common denominator," she whispered.

And there it was.

Not shame.

Not guilt.

Just clarity.

THE BREAKDOWN THAT BECAME A BREAK-THROUGH

Tanya told me how she'd stayed with her ex long after her gut screamed to leave.

She admitted that she lent her sister money to feel needed. She said she never told her boss what she wanted, just assumed he'd notice her efforts.

That's when she said it:

"Fu*k Me. I taught them how to treat me."

It wasn't self-blame—it was self-awareness.

She finally saw that *"Fu*k Them"* was step one.

But *"Fu*k Me"* was where the healing began.

That night, Tanya didn't make a vision board. She didn't light sage. She didn't do yoga poses named after jungle cats. She sat with the truth. She took ownership.

And the next morning, she did something wild—

She called her sister and set a real boundary. She sent her boss a resume with her two weeks' notice. She deleted her ex's number without announcing it on social media.

Nobody clapped.

Nobody liked it.

But *she* felt lighter than she had in years.

THE POWER OF "FU*K ME"

Now, months later, Tanya doesn't walk around angry anymore. She doesn't need to prove she's not to be messed with.

She knows.

And because she said "Fu*k Me" that one night, she gave herself the power back.

Not to change *them*. To change *her*.

She's dating again, but this time she walks away the second she sees a walking red flag.

She answers her sister's calls, but never her Venmo requests.

She's starting a business—and guess who's not invited? She-lia.

She told me, "Reid, I thought boundaries were about walls.

Turns out, they're just doors I forgot I could close."

So if you're reading this and thinking, "Damn, maybe I'm Tanya"...

Good.

That means you're awake.

You're not broken. You're not behind.

You're becoming.

Say it with me—

"Fu*k Them... but also, Fu*k Me."

FINAL WORDS FROM A WOMAN WHO'S BEEN IN THE MESSY MIDDLE

There is nothing braver than being honest with yourself.

There is nothing sexier than emotional maturity.

And there is nothing more revolutionary than saying, "I got me."

Not in a hashtag way.

In a call yourself out, clean your own mess, and still love yourself wildly kind of way.

You don't have to be perfect.

You just have to be done blaming people who don't even remember what they did.

So say it with me—loud, messy, and real:

Now say it with me:

"Fu*k Them."

"Fu*k Me."

You ready

Now let's go rebuild a life we actually want.

Chapter Three

Profanity Pilates

"The Art of Saying Fu*k Them:
A Speech Therapy Workshop for
the Emotionally Intelligent."

Let's be clear: *The Fu*k Them Theory isn't Sunday school material—and it's not meant to be. It's therapeutic, not theological.* Saying "Fu*k" is a pressure valve, not a spiritual declaration. For many of us, it's emotional triage—an instant, rebellious exhale that tells our nervous system, "I've got this." Research even shows swearing can reduce pain and stress, like a verbal ice pack for the soul. But I also get it—this language won't resonate with everyone. Whether it's religion, upbringing, or personal values, some people need a different kind of release. And that's okay. This theory isn't a sermon—it's a strategy. If "fu*k them" feels wrong to you, don't say it. But don't judge those of us who do, because for some of us, profanity *is* like a prayer.

It's the verbal pepper spray of personal boundaries. But here's the thing nobody teaches you in elementary school: you've got to use it right. You don't just toss around "fu*k them" like confetti at a pity party. You *craft* it. You *own* it. You *articulate* it. And by the time you're done with this chapter, you'll not only be fluent in one of the most beautiful emotional dialects ever created, you'll have better pronunciation than a Juilliard dropout trying to scream their way through Hamlet.

Welcome to Fu*k Them Speech Therapy 101.

PART ONE: THE LINGUISTICS OF LIBERATION

We are only working with eight letters: **F, U, C, K, T, H, E, M.** That's it. These are the building blocks of emotional freedom. We're working with a mi
nimal alphabet, but trust me—these are the only letters you'll need to survive your next family reunion, office team-building retreat, or unexpected Facebook message from your ex.

Let's get phonetic.

Phoneme Focus:
- **F** – The hiss of the boundary. Controlled. Fierce. Like letting the air out of a toxic balloon.
- **U** – The vowel of ownership. It's open, it's direct. You are not whispering anymore.
- **C** – The consonant that lands like a punch. Controlled aggression.
- **K** – The exhale. The sharpness. The dagger at the end.
- **T** – The tap. The knuckle knock before the "HELL no."
- **H** – The sigh before the warcry. The chest breath.
- **E** – The connective tissue. The bridge between fury and fact.
- **M** – The final hum of detachment. Satisfaction. Peace. Mic drop.

PART TWO: ARTICULATION DRILLS FOR THE PROFANE PROFESSIONAL

You wouldn't perform a deadlift without warming up, would you? (Okay, maybe you would, but that's why your boundaries are herniated.)

Exercise 1: Mirror Mouth Fu*kery

Instructions:
- Stand in front of a mirror.
- Look yourself in the eye like you just caught yourself texting back a narcissist.
- Say slowly and clearly:

Fuhh—kuh. Themm.

Repeat. Vary the emphasis.

o   "Fuhk them."

o   "Fuhk **THEM**."

o   "**FUHK**. Them."

o   Whisper it like a promise.

Scream it like your mental health depends on it (because sometimes, it does).

Exercise 2: Breath-Backed Boundaries

Instructions:
- Inhale deeply through your nose. Hold for 4 seconds. Exhale and say:

o   **"Ffffff…"**

o   Then: **"UHHHHH"** (drawn out, like you're shaking off a mistake).

o   Followed by a clipped: **"CK."**

o   Pause. Power pose.

Now add:

o   **"Them."** Like you're dropping their emotional control off a cliff.

This trains your diaphragm and your dignity.

Exercise 3: The Emotional Metronome

Say the full phrase, one beat per letter:

F – U – C – K – T – H – E – M

Again. But this time with rhythm. Snap your fingers on "F" and "T." Clap on "K" and "M." Congratulations. That's jazz hands for boundary setting.

FFFFFF UUCCC KK! THHHHEEMMM.!

Good job. Repeat over and over.

FFFFFF UUCCC KK! THHHHEEMMM.!

FFFFFF UUCCC KK! THHHHEEMMM.!

Try using different accents. The *Racist Hillbilly* is one of my favorites.

You could try a French accent if you want to be snooty.

PART THREE: F.T. ANAGRAM THERAPY

Let's turn emotional regulation into a word game.

Using only the letters F, U, C, K, T, H, E, M, try rearranging into micro-affirmations. Here are a few you're legally allowed to tattoo on your rib cage:

• **THE FU*K ME** – A reminder to take care of yourself before you go saving morons.

• **MUCK THE FET** – Sounds like gibberish? That's because not everything people say to you needs to make sense. Say it back to them and walk away. Bonus: they'll think you're in a cult.

• **FUM THE KECH** – Not a real phrase. Doesn't need to be. Profanity can be cathartic gibberish if the intention is clear.

Play with it. Create your own. Hang it on a wall. Embroider it on a throw pillow.

PART FOUR: THE FU*K-THEM TEST

Before you let loose your newfound profanity proficiency, you must pass the sacred Three-Part Test:

1. **Is it deserved?**

Are they truly crossing a line? Or are you just hungry and near your mother?

2. **Is it empowering?**

Are you saying it to take back your voice, or just to be petty?

3. **Is it private (or worth the fallout)?**

If you yell "FU*K THEM" in the conference room, are you ready to clean out your desk? Or better yet, are you excited about it?

PART FIVE: CLOSURE IN CURSING

You don't say **fu*k them** because you're mean. You say it because you've finally reached the part of your story where you stop explaining your worth to people who wouldn't notice your value if it hit them in the face holding a resume, a wedding ring, or a casserole dish.

Profanity—when used with purpose—isn't rude. It's *revolutionary.*

So take your limited alphabet. Train it. Speak it clearly. And never, ever apologize for saying what needed to be said.

If you can say this poem easily, you are a natural. Forget Pilates. You are Hall of Fame level.

"The Cussword Carousel"
(a tongue-twister poem for the verbally unhinged)

Flickin' filthy flapsnaps, Fred flung five f**ks,
Fast as a fox with a fistful of ducks.
Shifty shit-slingers shoved sharp slurs,
Snickering, snorting, snappin' curse-spurred slurs.

Bastardly Brenda banged ten damn drums,
While dickish Dan danced on Debbie's thumbs.
"C**t-cackling crows!" cried kooky old Kip,
As a tit-bitten toddler took one rude trip.

Hellbent on heckling, Hank howled "Hell!"
While prickly Pete picked pubes in a well.
"Assholes assemble!" screamed Sassy McSpite,
"Let's motherf*** mimes till the morning light!"

Butt-nugget Brenda belched a bold "b*tch,"
Then tripped on a turd and tumbled in pitch.
Screwball Steve screamed "suck it, you swine!"
While twirling two twats on a thorny clothesline.

Cuss-crusted chaos clapped back in a blur—
One f**k, two sh*ts, and a damn slur.
So if you're still standing, still slinging spit,
Say the whole damn thing—without losing your sh*t.

HOMEWORK:

1.   Stand in your kitchen with your Boston Terrier watching. Practice "Fu*k Them" with emotion, clarity, and eye contact.

2.   Write five new F-U-C-K-T-H-E-M phrases using only those eight letters. Post the best one on your fridge.

3.   Say the phrase silently every time someone tells you to "smile more."

4.   Record yourself saying it once. Save it. That's your emergency exit button from people-pleasing.

Learn how to say the *Silent* Fu*k Them. *Why saying it in your mind is actually more powerful than screaming it at Thanksgiving.*

Because growth is quiet—but the rehearsal can be loud.

Chapter Four

Fu*k Politics

Let me start with this: **thinking about politics is hazardous to your mental health.** I don't care how smart you are, how many "balanced sources" you subscribe to, or how loudly you shout, "I'm just staying informed!" You're not informing yourself. You're self-poisoning.

Politics is like emotional fentanyl. It's potent. It's addictive. And just a little bit will mess you up for days.

Here's what happens when you "just peek" at the news:

You wake up. You reach for your phone. Before your feet even touch the floor, you're already scrolling through a political car crash, watching strangers scream at each other in the comments section like it's WrestleMania for the socially constipated. You think you're "getting caught up." What you're actually doing is signing up to be emotionally hijacked before your coffee even has a chance to intervene.

Now you're angry. You're tense. You're arguing with a co-worker in your head who hasn't even said anything yet. Congratulations—you've just been politically possessed.

Why? Because politics isn't designed to inform you. It's designed to inflame you.

Look, I'm not saying "don't vote." I'm not saying "ignore the world." What I *am* saying is know the difference between being a citizen and being a sucker.

If your blood pressure goes up every time a politician breathes, that's not civic duty. That's a stress disorder with a campaign sign.

Here's a rule I live by:

If it doesn't affect your bank account, your body, or your bedtime—stop thinking about it.

Half of us are trapped in emotional hostage negotiations with people we've never met, over bills that haven't passed, involving rights that haven't been taken. And the kicker? Most of it's theater. A rage-fueled Netflix series where every season ends in the same mess it started with, except now you've lost three friendships and developed an eye twitch.

The truth no one wants to say out loud:

Thinking about politics all the time doesn't make you more informed.
It makes you more *performative.*
More *exhausted.*
More likely to scream at a barista over oat milk because you're "just sick of the government."

No, sweet pea. You're just over-caffeinated and under-boundaried.

Let's not pretend. Let's not play cute. Let's not slap on a performative bipartisan hug and pretend it's not a full-blown ideological bar fight out here.
Because if you've been anywhere near a Facebook comment section or accidentally walked into a Thanksgiving with a red state cousin, you know:

Democrats have a long, steamy, rage-fueled hate list when it comes to Republicans.

And before you get triggered, remember—I have a Ph.D. in Problem People Studies. This is not a drill. This is a diagnosis.

So grab your kombucha or your bourbon, depending on where your ass lands on the political spectrum, and let me walk you through exactly why Democrats wake up clenching their jaw at the word "Republican."

1. The Flag Fetish
You know the type. Truck nuts. Bald eagle tattoo. Six American flags per lawn.

To Democrats, it's not patriotism—it's performance art with delusion in red, white, and blue. Democrats hate that Republicans treat the flag like a personality. Because when you wave it in someone's face while trying to defund school lunches, it's not freedom. It's cosplay with a side of "don't tread on my empathy."

2. The Guns-Over-Everything Mindset
Democrats see a mass shooting and think: "This is horrific. Let's fix it." Republicans? They clutch their AR-15 like it's a childhood teddy bear. It's not about the Second Amendment—it's about the stubborn refusal to acknowledge basic math: more guns, more dead people. That's not complicated. That's kindergarten level "cause and effect."

3. The "My Religion Is the Law" Agenda
Jesus is great. But when Republicans turn Him into a lobbyist? That's where Democrats break out in hives. Republicans say "freedom of religion." But what they mean is "freedom to enforce mine." Democrats hate that. Because forcing Bible verses into legislation is not spiritual—it's strategic control dressed up as divine intervention.

4. The War on Woke (aka: Reading Books is Scary)
Republicans have rebranded basic human decency as "woke."

Empathy? Woke. Respecting trans people? Woke.

Teaching history that isn't Mayflower fan fiction? Extra woke.

Democrats hate that the bar is so low, you can trip over it in flip-flops.

5. The Denial Olympics

Climate change? Not real.

Systemic racism? Not real.

Insurrection? Tourists.

Republicans act like if they close their eyes long enough, the planet will stop melting and everyone will just forget about January 6th.

Democrats? They're in therapy over it. Republicans? They're in denial—on a jet ski.

6. The Weaponized Stupidity

Look—Democrats are not mad at dumb people.

They're mad at *strategically dumb people*.

The ones who deny science until they get COVID, then ask if the horse paste is vegan.

The ones who think Bill Gates is putting microchips in vaccine vials but can't name three branches of government.

It's not ignorance. It's weaponized nonsense, and Democrats are exhausted from explaining gravity to people who think the Earth is flat and feelings are facts.

7. The Hypocrisy Hangover

Democrats hate the double standards.

Family values? Until your candidate cheats with a porn star.

Law and order? Until your guy gets indicted.

Fiscal responsibility? Until you're throwing billions at border walls and golf trips.

It's not even the corruption that stings—it's the smugness

with which it's served.

8. The Faux-Victim Complex

Republicans act like saying "Happy Holidays" is an act of war.

Like Target selling a rainbow mug is an assassination attempt.

Democrats hate the constant crying wolf—because somewhere, actual wolves are out there, and we're too busy arguing about pronouns to notice

9. The Power Grab in a Democracy Costume

Gerrymandering. Voter suppression. Electoral gymnastics. Republicans say they love democracy.

But to Democrats, it feels more like they love winning—and if democracy has to choke in the backseat for that to happen, so be it.

It's not strategy. It's sabotage in a red tie.

So What the Fu*k Do We Do With This?

If you're a Democrat reading this, you're nodding so hard your neck just filed a restraining order.

If you're a Republican, you're already halfway through your angry reply and haven't blinked in four minutes.

But here's the Mel Robbins moment you didn't see coming:

Say it with me....Fu*k Them!!!

Let them be loud. Let them post memes in Comic Sans. Let them call empathy "elitism."

You can't fix delusion with logic. You can't fix hate with a factsheet.

You can only fix your own damn boundaries.

So, Democrat or not, ask yourself:

What are you tolerating that's keeping you stuck in outrage?

And what would happen if you just... didn't?

Let them stew. Let them shout.

Then go vote like your uterus, your planet, and your TikTok app depend on it.

Because they do.

The other side.

If you've ever been to a family cookout, a PTA meeting, or the comment section of a Facebook post about gas prices, you've probably heard a Republican say something like, *"The country's going to hell because of those damn Democrats."*

First of all, calm down, Craig. Second of all, let's get real: Republicans hate a lot of things about Democrats. Not like a gentle "I disagree with your policy on zoning regulations" kind of hate. I'm talking "toss-your-remote-through-the-TV-because-AOC-is-talking" hate.

So why? Why do they get that twitch in their eye every time they hear "equity" or "student loan forgiveness"? Let's break it down. Because knowledge is power. And also because if I hear one more person yell "I didn't vote for Elon" at a school board meeting, I'm going to start drinking boxed wine again.

1. Democrats Love Feelings

Republicans see Democrats the way a grizzly bear sees a vegan yoga instructor: confusing, underfed, and entirely too emotional.

Democrats want to *feel* their way through policy:

- "Let's make sure everyone feels heard."
- "We need to center marginalized voices."
- "No one should feel left out."

Meanwhile, Republicans are over here like:

"I didn't cry at my dad's funeral, I'm sure as hell not crying over your pronouns, Debra."

2. They Keep Making New Genders

Republicans miss the good old days when gender came in two options: *cowboy* or *cheerleader*.

They think Democrats wake up each morning, spin a rainbow wheel, and land on something like "pan-romantic mothperson." To them, it's not inclusive—it's *confusing*. And confusion feels threatening.

Also, they don't like being corrected. Nothing pisses off a Republican more than getting yelled at for saying "ma'am" at Tractor Supply.

3. Democrats Love Government Like It's a Sugar Daddy

To a Republican, the government is a necessary evil. To a Democrat, it's a benevolent giant with a checkbook and a therapy degree.

Democrats want:
- Free healthcare
- Free college
- Free tampons in men's bathrooms

Republicans hear this and scream, **"WHO'S PAYING FOR THIS?!"**

They say it louder when they're on their third Bud Light, even though they haven't paid taxes since 2011 because they registered their ATV dealership as a church.

4. They Won't Shut Up About Climate Change

"Eat less meat!"

"Stop using plastic straws!"

"Don't have eleven kids and drive a diesel Suburban, Cheryl!"

Republicans see this as personal. Like Democrats are coming for their God-given right to barbecue ribs on a gas grill while watering their lawn in a drought with a hose made of baby seals.

5. They Treat Everyone Like a Victim Except White Dudes

Democrats have built an entire platform around advocacy and justice.

Which sounds great—until you're the one getting labeled as the villain just for existing.

To Republicans, it feels like:
- You can't say anything without being "problematic."
- You can't joke without being "offensive."
- You can't breathe without being told you're "privileged."

They feel like every Democrat comes with a checklist and a warning label.

6. They Love Cancel Culture Like It's Their Job

If Republicans see "woke" as a cult, then cancel culture is their exorcism ritual.

Democrats believe in accountability. Republicans think accountability ends at taxes and starts sounding a lot like censorship when your uncle gets fired for tweeting something racist in 2009.

7. They Trust Science Too Much, Unless It's About Biology

This one's wild. Republicans will scream "TRUST THE SCIENCE" when you tell them men can have babies, and then two seconds later call climate change "a liberal scam funded by George Soros."

Democrats think science is sacred. Republicans think it's *selectively applied BS with a lab coat.*

8. They Hate America (According to Republicans)

Republicans believe in flags, guns, and telling everyone else to leave if they don't like it.

Democrats believe in:

- Reimagining policing
- Acknowledging past sins
- Asking why we still have statues of slave owners

Republicans interpret that as:

"You hate this country and probably want to replace the Star-Spangled Banner with Lizzo's Juice."

Say it with me....Fu*k Them!!!

FINAL WORD FROM REID

Here's the truth: Republicans don't really hate Democrats.

They hate what Democrats make them feel: uncertain, old-fashioned, and out of control.

They hate being wrong.

They hate being called out.

They hate the idea that maybe—just maybe—the world is changing and they didn't get the memo.

But hate? That's just fear dressed up in a bald eagle tank top.

And fear doesn't get to drive your life.

Unless you're in Florida.

Then fear has a driver's license, a gun, and probably runs your school board.

So what's the solution? Stop scrolling. Stop debating your cousin on Facebook. Stop yelling at the TV like it owes you reparations.

And instead?

Go vote. Go volunteer. Go live.

Then? Go take a damn nap. That's real activism. That's real resistance. Because they want you distracted. Angry. Depleted.

But you? You're smarter than that.You're not a pawn. You're not a pundit.

Chapter Five

Fu*k Family Drama

Let me start with this: I love my family. I also once locked myself in a Dollar Tree bathroom for forty-five minutes just to avoid helping my cousin make a "vision board for her divorce." Family is sacred. Family is psycho.

And here's the part no one teaches you in Sunday School:

You are not responsible for being the emotional janitor of your family's bullsh*t.

Let them spiral. Let them stew. Let them burn sage in their basements and misquote Brené Brown in a group chat. Not your problem.

Exhibit A: My Sister and the Trauma Olympics

My sister *Meghan-with-an-H* once organized a family Zoom meeting titled **"Emergency: Reid's Vibe."** The agenda? Apparently, I had "bad energy" for missing her daughter's third-grade Earth Day recital.

Let me be clear: *her daughter was a recycling bin.* Literally. A box with googly eyes.

Meghan made slides. Slides. One of them said, "The Erosion of Sisterhood: A Timeline."

She also included a pie chart titled *"How Often Reid Texts Back (And How That Hurts Us Spiritually)."*

I said Fu*k Her. I muted the Zoom, drank a mimosa, and crocheted a hat for my Boston Terrier.

Let her host the PowerPoint Pity Parade. I am not the keynote speaker at her delusion conference.

Exhibit B: Uncle Dave and the Witch Hunt for Mental Health

Uncle Dave thinks therapy is a government trap. He also once shot his own mailbox because it "looked suspicious." Every family dinner, he arrives wearing camouflage and rage.

This past Thanksgiving, he pointed a turkey leg at me and said:

"Your whole job is just telling people their mommy didn't hug them right. That's not science. That's bullshit."

I used to argue. Now I just say, "You're absolutely right, Dave. Now please pass the emotional stuffing."

Let him think my Ph.D. is a pentagram. Let him write his memoirs in beef jerky. I've stopped enrolling in the madness.

Exhibit C: My Mother and the Guilt Oscars

And then... there's my mother. Queen of Silent Judgments. Duchess of Loaded Statements. Empress of the Guilt-Trip Economy.

When I told her I wasn't coming home for Easter last year because I had two kids with strep throat, she said—dead serious:

"Well. Jesus still made it to the resurrection."

The woman taped a note to her front door that read:

"Some daughters rise. Others sleep in and abandon their mothers."

Another time, she sent me a card that said, *"Thinking of you,"* and inside it was just a photo of her standing next to my childhood bedroom holding a single wilted daffodil. Like she was filming an indie movie about maternal neglect.

Old me would've packed up guilt and driven through a snowstorm to cut ham for people who think boundaries are rude.

New me texted: "Nice lighting in the photo. Happy Easter, Mom."

Fu*k her emotional theater. I'm not auditioning for her one-woman show titled "Why Reid Hurts Me Most."

Here's the Gospel Truth

Your family's dysfunction is not a sacred relic. You don't have to preserve it. You don't have to decode it. And you damn sure don't have to participate in it.

Let them act out. Let them have tantrums with PowerPoint. Let them write cryptic Facebook statuses that say, "Some people forget who bought them their first calculator."

You? You're done being the crisis concierge.

Let them misunderstand you. Let them host brunches without you. Let them whisper. Let them bake casseroles of resentment.

You go do what you were put here to do: live in peace, tell the truth, and raise a middle finger in love and liberation.

Fu*k the family drama.

Look, I know what you want me to say. That love is always equal. That every child is a sunbeam of equal wattage. That I tuck them both in with the same Disney+ infused affection.

But I won't say that. Because it's a lie. And you know it.

Here's the truth:

Sometimes you love one kid more than the other.

And sometimes—it's because one of them is just... easier to love.

The Bad Seed Theory

There. I said it.

Some kids are like emotional Labradors. They bring snacks to your bedside. They color within the lines. They apologize when they burp.

And others?

Others are walking Reddit threads. Constant drama. Wildly inconvenient opinions. They punch holes in your drywall and then cry because their "vibe was disrespected."

I had one of each.

And yes, I FELT THE GUILT.

I would rock the sweet one a little longer. I'd text back faster. I'd show up with snacks.

And then I'd look at the other one—the one who once called me "mid" in public—and I'd wonder if I was a monster.

But then I realized something.

Guilt Is Not a Moral Compass.

It's a smoke alarm.

And honey, you can't live your life in a kitchen full of burnt toast and pretend nothing's on fire. You feel guilty because you know your behavior is leaning. But that doesn't mean the kid isn't a nightmare sometimes.

And here's where I drop the truth bomb, straight from my Ph.D. in Problem People Studies:

You don't owe your kids a fake personality.

You owe them honesty.

And that includes honest frustration, exhaustion, and—yes— imbalanced love in the moment.

"But That's So Unfair!"

Yeah, well so is life.

So is childbirth.

So is that kid stealing your last Little Debbie and blaming the dog.

You are not required to pretend that emotional equity is always possible.

You are required to keep showing up.

You are required to love them both, in different ways, at different times, depending on who's being less of a shit that week.

You are not required to make it look perfect.

The Radical Solution: Let Them Be the One

Let one be the golden child for a season.

Let the other one stew in their teenage villain arc.

Let yourself admit it without branding your soul a bad parent.

Because here's what happens when you stop pretending: You parent better. You breathe deeper. And the kid who's testing every boundary? They finally see your humanity.

Which—ironically—is what usually makes them stop being such a raging jerk.

So the next time you're sipping coffee while your favorite child quietly reads a book and the other one is melting down because "nobody gets their aesthetic," just smile, and say to yourself,

"And also... Fu*k Them Damn Kids."

I know that was hard to say, hard to imagine, too cruel. But, didn't it feel good saying it?

You haven't truly lived until your mom accidentally (read:

very much on purpose) posts a 400-word essay on Facebook about your "rebellious phase," complete with a blurry photo of you in fishnet tights, carrying a bottle of Sprite she *absolutely* insists was vodka.

I was sitting at my kitchen table, half-dressed in ambition and a caffeine crash, when the group chat started pinging like the apocalypse. It was my old church ladies group—women with names like Darla and Phyllis and "Sister Bev"—the type who crochet Bible verses into pillows and still comment "Amen" under car accident posts.

My mother, bless her highly selective memory, had just posted:

"Please pray for my daughter Reid. She used to be such a good girl before college and her 'identity crisis.' I remember when she wore skirts below the knee and respected men. Now she yells 'feminism' and wears tattoos and pants with holes. Also, her dog has an Instagram. So sad what higher education does."

She tagged me.

She. TAGGED. Me. I didn't teach her that.

And the photo? I was mid-bite into a corndog. There was no escaping the shame. It was already shared seventeen times. Pastor Rick commented with a single candle emoji.

Now look, my first instinct was to throw my phone in a blender and start a new life as a waitress in Guam. But then I remembered: **Fu*k her.** Let my mom post that mortifying novella. Let her remind everyone I used to be in the church nativity play before I got a doctorate in Problem People Studies and told the world to "Fu*k Them." Let her tag the entire congregation and Aunt Trudy in Oklahoma. Why?

Because if you're out here trying to live a bold, authentic, joyful life—someone's gonna have a problem with it. And sometimes that "someone" is the woman who once grounded you for rolling your eyes during a Hillsong song.

You don't need to go into comment battle mode. You don't need to issue a formal PR apology to the Ladies Prayer Facebook group. And you definitely don't need to explain to your mom what a trauma response actually is.

You just need say...fu*k them."

Let them say it. Let them post it. Let them believe what they need to believe so they can sleep at night in their ruffled pillow shams and matching pajama sets from QVC.

Because you? You're not here to be understood.

You're here to *thrive* in spite of it.

So the next time someone drops your name in a post meant to "bring you back to the Lord" or blasts your spiritual downfall to 84 mutuals—fu*k them.

And then go back to building your legacy in sweatpants with your dog influencer and your PhD. Because that, my friend, is peace.

And if your mother sends you a poem she "just happened to write" about daughters who forget Mother's Day? Print it out. Frame it. Place it in the bathroom.

Next to the plunger.

Look, I'm not here to sprinkle glitter on a turd and call it transformation. I'm a cynic. A realist with a Ph.D. in Problem People. I don't believe everyone is good deep down. Some people are just chaos with eyebrows. And honestly? That's fine. Let them rot in their own mess. I've seen too much to slap a motivational poster over dysfunction and call it healing. Life isn't a damn Hallmark card. It's survival. And if I have to be the morbid voice in your ear reminding you that not everyone deserves access to your peace? So be it.

Chapter Six

CoWorkers, Fu*k Them Too

Do you remember Alissa Heinerscheid? She was the key figure behind what was referred to as the "Bud Light disaster," which involved a significant decline in sales following a sponsored post with transgender influencer Dylan Mulvaney. At that time, Heinerscheid was Bud Light's vice president of marketing and was often blamed for the decision. However, it's important to note that the collaboration with Mulvaney was a result of a team effort. The was a billion-dollar mistake.

Imagine the CEO from Budweiser sitting stiffly at the end of the conference room table, nodding like a bobblehead as the marketing team unveiled what would go down as one of the worst ad campaigns in brand history. Deep down, his gut screamed Fu*k Them—every smug strategist, every slide of woke nonsense—but he swallowed it, hard. He smiled politely, let the bad idea ride, and convinced himself it would "play well with younger demos." He didn't have the balls to speak the truth, and that cowardice cost the company millions and nearly torched a legacy built on beer, ball games, and backyard barbecues. But, he is the CEO. He should've screamed *Fu*k Them*, but...he didn't.

You might think Fu*k Them all day long—every time your coworker takes credit for your idea, when your boss schedules a 4:59 p.m. meeting, or when Carol from HR reminds you about the dress code while she's in flip-flops—but here's the deal: saying it out loud at work can cost you more than your sanity. Speaking your mind in the wrong setting can get you labeled "unprofessional," "difficult," or worse, "no longer employed." I'm not saying don't have boundaries—I wrote the damn book on that—but just know, if you broadcast your internal monologue to the break room, the next meeting you attend might be your exit interview.

Let's get one thing straight. Work would be amazing if it weren't for the people. That's right. It's not the deadlines, the PowerPoints, or the 8 a.m. meetings that break your spirit — it's the coworkers.

Bad coworkers come in three flavors:

1. Ignorant like it's a superpower.
2. Backstabby with a smile.
3. Kiss-asses so shiny they practically squeak when they walk.

Let's unpack.

THE IGNORANT ONES: *"I Didn't Know" Is Their Life Motto*

There's always that person. The one who somehow doesn't know how email works, forgets every single training, and spends half the day asking, "Wait, what are we supposed to be doing?"

Fu*k Them.

Let them be confused. Let them float through the workday like a sentient bag of trail mix. Let them miss the memo, the meeting, the point.

You can't fix stupid at work — and you shouldn't waste your energy trying.

I used to correct them. Send helpful links. Offer to "walk them through it." What did I get? Blamed when they still messed it up. Labeled "bossy." One even called me "a know-it-all with boundary issues." (Which, okay, true. But I was *right*, dammit.)

Now? I smile. I let them fall on their PowerPoint swords. I sip my coffee while watching their presentation combust like a toaster in a bathtub.

Because here's the thing: just because you work with them doesn't mean you owe them clarity.

Let them be clueless. Protect your bandwidth. Fu*k Them.

THE BACKSTABBERS: *Death By A Thousand CCs*

Here's the trickiest kind of coworker — *the professional hand-raiser who shivs you in the copy room*. You know them. They smile during team meetings, then forward your mistakes to management faster than a rumor spreads on Slack.

I once had a colleague — we'll call her *Tammy Two-Faced* — who made passive-aggressiveness into a career path. One minute she's complimenting my outfit, next she's telling my boss that I "seem overwhelmed and maybe shouldn't lead the client meeting."

She was a spreadsheet in the streets, sabotage in the sheets.

My old self would've panicked. Apologized. Over-explained. Tried to win her over with baked goods and LinkedIn endorsements.

But now? I activate my Fu*k Them Filter.

You don't win against a backstabber by fighting dirty. You win by staying clean and letting receipts speak louder than rumors. Screenshot. Save. Document. And when the drama hits the fan, you walk in calm, collected, and covered in CYA emails.

Let them scheme. Let them gossip. Let them build their paper mache empire of lies.

You stay focused, excellent, and just petty enough to block them on Teams.

THE KISS-ASSES: *Professional Lip Gloss Users*

Ah, the ass-kissers. These are the people who act like your boss is God's gift to corporate strategy. They clap at every idea. They nod so hard you worry about neck injuries. They write thank-you notes for Monday morning emails.

Fu*k Them.

They think success is about brown-nosing. You know better. Because here's the secret: real leadership isn't looking for sycophants. It's looking for people who solve problems, not people who laminate compliments.

Let them overdo it. Let them book "coffee chats" with the VP and post it on LinkedIn. Let them submit project ideas that are just repackaged bullet points from last week's meeting.

You? You stay real. Authentic. Respectful — but not rehearsed.

When they're out here throwing praise like Mardi Gras beads, you stay focused on delivering results and not losing your damn self in the process.

Let me be crystal-clear: I've had bosses who inspired me, bosses who ignored me, and bosses who treated me like a human Post-it—useful only for reminders and easily discarded.

Bosses can be empowering, infuriating, or just... there, like a potted plant with a corporate email address.

But here's the most liberating truth no one teaches you in business school:

Your boss is not your parent.

They're not your therapist, your savior, or your moral compass.

They're just a human being with a title, a calendar full of meetings, and probably an overinflated sense of self-worth because someone once called them "a visionary" during an offsite.

THE BURNOUT BOOMERANG

Let's talk about burnout — yours, not theirs, because trust me, they're fine. They're on vacation every other month "recharging," while you're over here recharging your laptop at 2 a.m. to finish a slide deck no one will read.

You stay late. You take on extra projects. You answer emails from the shower. Why?

Because you think hard work = promotions = validation.

But here's the kicker: burnout isn't a badge of honor — it's a warning sign.

Your ambition doesn't need to die, but your obsession with proving yourself to people who wouldn't notice if you got hit by a printer? Yeah, that can go.

Let them pile it on. Let them act like boundaries are for interns and bathroom breaks are luxuries.

You say no. You log off. You live.

THE PROMOTION LOTTERY

You know how the promotion process works? It doesn't.

It's not a system. It's a *slot machine with a broken handle,* and your best odds are being seen — not just being good.

And even then? They still might promote Brad who golfs and barely knows what the company does.

Fu*k Them.

Let them pick the unqualified dude in chinos with a firm handshake and zero charisma.

You? You keep receipts. You keep improving. You build relationships *outside* the org chart. And if it never happens? You leave. Proudly. With your head high and your mental health intact.

THE POWER SHIFT

When you start working like your boss isn't the sun around which your life orbits, everything changes.

You stop chasing approval.

You start honoring your capacity.

You stop taking feedback like scripture.

You start treating it like a buffet — take what nourishes, leave the crap with raisins in it.

Let them micromanage. Let them ignore your ideas. Let them hog the credit in meetings while you're in the background rolling your eyes so hard it burns calories. "Fu*k Them Assholes!"

You weren't hired to be a cheerleader, a therapist, or a scapegoat.

You were hired to work. And that's exactly what you'll do — with integrity, dignity, and just enough pettiness to keep things interesting.

FINAL THOUGHT:

You don't go to work to fix people.

You go to work to do your job, protect your peace, and get paid.

So Fu*k Them.

Let the clueless spin. Let the snakes slither. Let the bootlickers polish every damn heel in the building.

Because when you stop trying to change the clowns and start acting like the damn ringleader, you'll find something amazing:

They don't have power unless you hand it to them.

So the next time you feel triggered by a ridiculous coworker? Pause. Breathe.

And say the magic words:

Fu*k. Them.

Chapter Seven

People Never Change.
Use Passive Aggressive Torturing.

Changing people is like trying to iron a shirt that's still on the hanger—awkward, frustrating, and ultimately useless. I've wasted years thinking the right argument, tone, or tearful plea would finally get my spouse to listen, my adult children to grow up, my friends to act right, or my coworkers to be less petty. But here's the truth: people don't change because you want them to. They change because *they* want to—or not at all. No matter how logical your case or how noble your intentions, if they're not ready, willing, and actively working on it, your efforts will fall flat. You'll just end up exhausted, resentful, and possibly in therapy for "communication fatigue."

If you have no chance of changing them, my theory suggests that you might as well benefit for your own piece of mind. I will explain.

Let's be honest. Sometimes, the people we love the most make life choices that are so baffling, you start to wonder if you actually gave birth to a barnacle or married a sofa cushion with vocal cords. And as much as I preach the gospel of the

—release control, stop fixing people, mind your own damn business—it doesn't mean you're a monk floating above the chaos in a cloud of lavender-scented detachment.

You're human. With stress. Rage. Sighs so deep they come from a past life. And when deep breathing isn't cutting it, and wine at noon is frowned upon (by people we don't trust anyway),

I want to give you a gentle, effective, and delightfully evil form of stress relief:

Passive-Aggressive Torturing.

Not *real* torture. Not illegal stuff. I'm talking about emotional mosquito bites. The kinds that make *you* feel better while slowly chipping away at the entitled egos of the sloths you live with. You can come up with your own ways and make it better.

Here's some exambles.

The Lazy Husband: Dead Batteries, Dead Dreams

He won't mow the lawn. Won't fix the cabinet door that's been hanging like a drunk limb since last May. He will, however, spend six consecutive hours rewatching *Fast & Furious 4-8* because "he needs a break."

Here's your solution: keep a Ziploc bag full of already dead AA batteries. Every time his remote dies, offer your little baggie of "fresh ones." Smile like a Stepford wife and watch as he furiously smacks the remote like it's cheating on him.

Bonus Points: Whisper "that's weird" while you dust near him with unnecessary drama.

The Teenage Daughter: Unplugged and Unapologetic

She rolled her eyes when you reminded her to study. She called your favorite sweater "vintage" in that tone. And she left the back door open all night like raccoons pay rent.

Unplug her charger. Just a smidge every night. Not completely. Just enough that the charging symbol blinks, then disappears. She'll wake up with 6% and a full day of high school boy gossip to record.

Bonus Points: Say, "Hmm. You probably didn't plug it in right," with the same expression she gives you when you use slang incorrectly.

The Mother-in-Law: Queen of Judgment

She comments on your parenting. She comments on your cooking. She breathes like she's allergic to your existence.

Send her a Christmas card in June. Write "Thanks for being such an unforgettable presence in our lives. We still talk about last Thanksgiving." Then sign it with an obviously forged version of her son's name. Watch the confusion spiral.

Bonus Points: Include a family photo where she's almost cropped out.

Other ideas:
1. Set his/her wake alarm wrong.
2. Fold his socks all mis-matched.
3. Search for porn on his computer, and accuse him.
4. Ruin his/her favorite clothes with bleech in the laudry.
5. Accidenty burn his favorite meal, or make it wrong.
6. Leave only dried out pens in her/his desks.
7. Replace full toothpaste tubes with empty ones.
8. Wear a perfume/colonge you know he/she hates.
9. Hide something everyday. Keys, phone, dog leash.
10. And farting beside him/her is always a classic

Why This Works

You're not out here slashing tires or poisoning the chili. You're restoring balance. You're emotionally exfoliating. These little acts of passive-aggressive rebellion are like putting glitter in the cracks of your sanity—they make it sparkle.

Here's the truth: you can't force people to live differently. You can't strap ambition to your husband's back or replace your daughter's attitude with gratitude. You can, however, remind yourself that you're still in control of how much of their chaos you're willing to absorb. And sometimes, when you feel powerless, giving them just a little hiccup in their entitled day is all it takes to soothe your inner riot.

Remember: this is not about revenge. It's about regulation. Emotional balance. Passive-aggressive torture is the adult woman's essential oil. Use it sparingly, use it wisely, and always keep a bag of dead batteries handy.

Because sometimes "Fu*k Them" isn't shouted—it's whispered as you unplug a charger with the grace of a woman who's done giving free therapy to people who won't even refill the Brita.

Namaste, baby.

Now go hide the TV remote.

Here are 10 passive-aggressive comments that a parent might drop on social media aimed at their teenage daughter—subtle, biting, and just salty enough to sting without being grounded-worthy:

1.   "So proud of my daughter for finding time to post selfies between ignoring my texts."

2.   "Love watching my teenager discover the thrill of reinventing things I did in 1998 like it's brand new."

3.   "Glad to see my daughter still has strong thumbs from texting, since lifting a dish is clearly too much."

4.   "Teenagers these days have such confidence... especially when they're wrong."

5.   "Nothing warms a mother's heart like hearing her daughter laugh—just wish it happened at home and not only on Snapchat."

6.   "Shoutout to my daughter for keeping her bedroom a mystery. Even archaeologists wouldn't go in there."

7. "Apparently the WiFi does work when I talk, but only when I stop, right?"

8. "So nice that my daughter is 'too busy' to help with chores but has a 7-part TikTok series about her skincare routine."

9. "Teenagers: because eye rolls and deep sighs are obviously a love language."

10. "She says I'm so embarrassing online—but here she is borrowing my mascara, my shampoo, my sanity..."

Here are some creative, sharp-edged, and slightly over-the-top examples of ways parents can sabotage their daughter's relationship with a loser guy—the kind who "forgets" his wallet, calls her "crazy" when she's right, and thinks ambition is a pyramid scheme:

1. The Subtle Background Campaign
Slip in phrases like, "Oh, he's still trying to get that Twitch channel off the ground?" at dinner. Bonus points for a concerned eyebrow raise.

2. The Job Listing Email Bombardment
Send her links to real jobs every morning titled:
"In case [INSERT LOSER'S NAME] wants to contribute to society today"
Attach a résumé template. Include a YouTube tutorial on punctuality.

3. The "Surprise" Credit Check Dinner
Invite him over for a fancy dinner. Mid-meal, casually bring up how you "ran his credit score for fun." Slide a printout across the table like you're at the Pentagon.

4. The Home Video Playback
Dig up childhood footage of her being smart, sassy, ambi-

tious—and then pan over to him sitting on the couch, barefoot, explaining why crypto is "just misunderstood." Ask: "Sweetheart, this is who you were. Where did she go?"

5. Weaponized Grandma

Unleash the unfiltered family elder. Let Grandma ask questions like:

- "Do you always wear a hat indoors, or is that court-ordered?"
- "What exactly is a vibe consultant?"
- "Is that a new face tattoo, or is that mold?"

6. The LinkedIn Intervention

Create a fake LinkedIn profile for him—filled with embarrassing lies like "former assistant to the assistant fry cook" and "aspiring DJ with two SoundCloud followers." Let her find it "by accident."

7. The Future Vision Board

Craft a "vision board" of her life if she stays with him: a trailer, seven broken down scooters, her working three jobs while he's gaming in pajama pants. Hang it on the fridge like kindergarten art.

8. The Generous Car Bribe

"Oh, he can't drive you because his tags are expired again? We were just thinking of getting you a car if you were, you know… single."

9. The Group Text Sabotage

Start a group chat with your daughter and all her exes. Name it:

"Men Who At Least Had Health Insurance."

Let it simmer.

10. The Casual Guest Speaker Night

Invite successful women over—lawyers, artists, engineers—and let them "accidentally" share stories of their loser-ex-boyfriend phases. Watch the wheels turn in your daughter's head.

Chapter Eight

Fu*k the Apology Tour

Let me say this louder for the people in the back: **you don't owe the internet an apology for who you are or what you think.** Not for being white. Not for loving Trump. Not for *hating* Trump. And certainly not for thinking *Hamilton* was overrated, overpriced, and overhyped. (Spoiler: it was.)

There's a weird trend happening out there — a pathological need to soften every opinion with a bow-tied apology. We're so afraid of cancelation, confrontation, or Karen-fueled backlash that we start every sentence with, "Sorry, but..." like we're trying to tiptoe through a minefield of feelings. Guess what? You're not a landmine. You're a person.

Let's break it down:

You Don't Owe an Apology for Being White

Let's just say it — melanin levels don't determine moral character. The world doesn't need another "I'm sorry I was born" soliloquy. Being white doesn't make you the villain in everyone else's origin story. And apologizing for your skin color isn't allyship — it's performance. If you want to be a good human, be kind, speak up when it matters, and stop acting like you need to atone for history you didn't write.

You Don't Owe an Apology for Who You Voted For

Whether you own a red hat or a Kamala bumper sticker, you've probably been told you're the reason democracy is on fire. **Newsflash: voting isn't a sin.** Loving Trump doesn't mean you're a white nationalist, and hating him doesn't make you an

America-hating socialist. We are allowed to disagree without someone demanding your resignation from society.

You don't have to follow that post-election script: "I voted for him, but I swear I'm not like *that.*" You don't need to distance yourself from your own convictions just to make brunch more comfortable for your yoga instructor cousin. If you believe what you believe, own it. Let them clutch their pearls — you're too busy living your life.

You Don't Owe an Apology for Hating "Hamilton"

The musical where the founding fathers are somehow all young, hot rappers in ponytails? Hamilton may have changed theater forever, but that doesn't mean you're obligated to worship it. If you'd rather sit through a root canal than hear one more syllable of "The Room Where It Happens," guess what? That's your right.

Liking something "problematic" doesn't make you problematic. Not liking something "beloved" doesn't make you a hater. You're not required to fake enthusiasm to fit in with the cultural choir.

The Bottom Line: You're Allowed to Exist Without Explaining Yourself

Not everything needs a preface. Not every truth needs to be bubble-wrapped in disclaimers. It's okay to have beliefs that are messy. Opinions that are unpopular. Preferences that are off-brand. *You don't need to apologize to strangers for being a complex human being.*

So, next time you feel that reflex creeping in — that urge to soften your truth, cave to the mob, or explain your soul — take a breath and say the magic words:

"F*ck Them. I'm not sorry."

Let me guess—you're tired of feeling like you owe everyone an explanation. An apology. A disclaimer. A thirty-minute talk every time you choose yourself over their expectations.

I see you.

I *was* you.

Welcome to the part of the book where I grab you by the shoulders, look you square in the eye, and say,

You don't need a podium.

You don't need a script.

You don't need their permission to change your damn life.

Stop Explaining Your Peace.

You left the toxic group chat. You ghosted the third cousin who only calls when they need money for "essential oils." You said no to brunch with people who drain your soul like a phone battery in a dead zone.

And now your brain is doing cartwheels trying to "make it right."

"Should I text them back?"

"Was I too harsh?"

"Maybe I should explain..."

No, babe. You should not.

I once left a committee at church that had more drama than an episode of Real Housewives of Boise. And what did I do after I left? I sent a 12-paragraph email explaining my "heart," my "journey," and my "hope to remain connected." You know what I got back?

Nothing.

Crickets.

One "thumbs-up" emoji and someone else taking credit for

the bake sale I planned.

I wasted hours—hours—crafting that essay. I could've used that time to exfoliate, meditate, or scream into a pillow. Instead, I drafted an Oscar-worthy apology to people who weren't even invested in my well-being.

Lesson: Silence is not rude. It's sacred.

The Truth About People Who Need an Explanation

Let me tell you a story about Sheila. Sheila was a friend of mine. Kind of. You know the type—gives you backhanded compliments like, "I admire how you're so comfortable not wearing makeup."

Sheila loved the old version of me. The over-functioning, people-pleasing, boundaryless doormat who always RSVP'd "yes" to every invite, even funerals for people I hadn't met.

So when I started saying "no," setting boundaries, not responding to passive-aggressive texts immediately—Sheila got triggered.

She said I owed her an explanation.

No, Sheila. I owed you a thank you for showing me who you really were.

You see, people who demand an explanation are rarely seeking clarity.

They're seeking control.

They want you to dance back into the version of you that made their life easier.

And I'm here to tell you:

Fu*k their ease. Claim your peace.

What Happens When You Stop Explaining

Your life gets louder in the places that matter.

Your joy gets thicker. Your sleep gets deeper. Your boundaries get Teflon-coated.

Do you know what happened when I stopped issuing apology statements like I worked for a PR firm? I had energy. Real, actual energy. The kind that makes you walk into Target and only buy what you came for.

I stopped worrying about "what they'll think" and started asking "what do I want?"

And here's the wild part: the people who truly love you—who see you—don't require a PowerPoint to understand your evolution.

They don't need you to justify your healing.

But What If I Hurt Someone?

Read this slowly:

There's a difference between hurting someone and disappointing their expectations of you.

You're not the villain because you changed.

You're not a monster because you grew.

You're not the bad guy because you left the group chat, the relationship, the church, the job, or the mother-in-law's weekly pot roast dinner.

Growth will always feel like betrayal to the people who benefited from your lack of boundaries.

So yes, they might feel "hurt"—but that doesn't mean you owe them a ticket to your soul's press conference. Sometimes the kindest thing you can do is let the silence speak.

The "Fu*k the Apology Tour" Manifesto

Here's what I want you to do. Write this down. Tape it to your bathroom mirror. Tattoo it on your frontal lobe. Whisper it to yourself before every Zoom meeting with people who don't know how to mute themselves:

1. I do not owe an explanation for protecting my energy.
2. I do not need permission to grow.
3. I will not apologize for being unavailable to chaos.
4. My no is a full sentence and a complete thought.
5. If you need me to explain who I am now, you probably never saw me clearly before.

Final Story: The Apology I Didn't Give

Years ago, I walked out of a business partnership. It was toxic. High-functioning dysfunction. My gut screamed run, and for once, I listened. I didn't send a long email. I didn't beg for understanding. I simply said: "This no longer works for me."

They said I was unprofessional.

They smeared my name.

They said I'd regret it.

I didn't.

Not for a single damn second.

That was the moment I finally stopped groveling for grace in rooms I didn't belong in.

I didn't give them the performance.

I didn't give them the postmortem.

I gave myself permission.

And that—right there—is the invitation I'm handing you.

Cancel the Apology Tour. Pack your bags. Get on the Peace Plane. First class only.

Because baby,

your explanation days are over.

So you did it. You walked off the Apology Tour like Beyoncé strutting off stage at Coachella—no mic drop needed. Just power, boundaries, and maybe a little bit of side-eye.

But now?

The air feels... different.

The silence is louder.

People are talking.

People are pulling back.

People are confused, offended, and saying things like:

- "She's changed."
- "He thinks he's better than us now."
- "They're so full of themselves lately."

Here's what I want you to do with all of that: Nothing.

What Happens After You Stop Explaining

The real detox isn't cutting people off. It's what happens after. It's the space. The awkward middle. The part where you want to sprint back to old habits just to fill the silence.

When I stopped apologizing for everything—my goals, my opinions, my time, my wrinkles—people fell into three categories:

1.   The Supporters – They clapped, said "about damn time," and handed me wine.

2.   The Confused – They didn't get it, but they still loved me. They watched from a distance with a raised eyebrow and a hesitant "you good?"

3.   The Offended – They went full blackout. Ghosted me. Blocked me on Facebook and Pinterest. Wrote passive-aggressive posts about "loyalty" and "fake friends."

Here's the truth:

Not everyone will come with you.

Not *everyone* should.

You Are Not Responsible for Their Reaction

Let me say this like I'm standing on your kitchen table in high heels:

You are not the emotional janitor for other people's feelings.

Their confusion is not your cue to over-explain.

Their anger is not your responsibility to soothe.

Their gossip is not your sign to clean up what they shattered.

You do not have to follow them into their emotional basement just because they're yelling from the stairs.

The Fallout Is a Filter

You think you're losing people. But really, you're just finally seeing them.

Let me tell you about Candice. Sweet, church-going, bible-verse-posting Candice who "just wanted to help." When I started shifting how I moved in the world—declining events, setting deadlines, charging for my work—Candice lost her holy mind.

She said I was "becoming worldly."

She said I had a potty mouth.

She said I "used to be more humble."

She said I needed to "pray about my attitude."

No, Candice. I needed to pray about your access to me.

She wasn't mad at my growth—she was mad she couldn't *benefit* from my lack of boundaries anymore.

The fallout was hard. But looking back, it was holy.

Because it filtered the fake support from the real.

The conditional love from the unconditional.

The clingy from the connected.

The Guilt Hangover Is Real (But Temporary)

Let's talk about the emotional hangover. You'll feel it. I promise. The first time you say "no" a
nd don't follow it with three paragraphs of apology? You'll lie in bed wondering if you're a monster.

You're not.

You're detoxing from years—*decades*—of conditioning.
People-pleasing withdrawal is real.
But every time you survive it?
Every time you sit in that guilt and *don't act on it?*
You rewire your brain to understand this powerful truth:
You are allowed to be misunderstood and still be good.

Fallout Isn't Failure. It's Freedom.

You're not failing because people walk away. You're not failing because someone is upset you stopped answering their 11 p.m. vent sessions. You're not failing because your group text dried up like an old sponge.
You're free.
Free to be yourself without writing a thesis.
Free to change without warning.
Free to shift, evolve, transform, burn bridges, and never check if the ashes formed a nice Instagram-worthy quote.
So What Do You Say When They Come Knocking?
Because sometimes, they do.
Sometimes the people who disappeared during your shift circle back.

They say things like:
- "You've been distant."
- "We miss the old you."
- "You just cut me off."

Here's your script. Ready?

"I made decisions that were right for me. I understand if that upset you, but I'm not going to apologize for it."

And then—this is important—you stop talking.
Let the silence sit like a warm casserole of awkward truth.

Final Story: The Bridge That Didn't Burn

Let me end with this: not all fallout is permanent.
One of my closest friends ghosted me for seven years. Why? Because I stopped being her emotional service animal. I stopped taking her crisis calls. I stopped cleaning up her messes.
We didn't speak.
Then one day, she called me. "I get it now," she said. "I didn't back then. But I do now. And I'm sorry."
That bridge? It didn't burn.
It just closed for maintenance.

Sometimes people come back. Sometimes they don't. But you? You don't sit in the rubble waiting. You build the life you want. You set the boundary. You light the sage.

You say:
"If the bridge stays burned, I'll build a boat."

Chapter Nine

Fu*k Them Assholes

OK, I didn't write this, but it is deadly accurate.

In contemporary social psychology and interpersonal discourse, the term "asshole" denotes an individual whose habitual patterns of entitlement, insensitivity, and deliberate disregard for the well-being of others create a hostile or toxic environment.

Unlike momentary rudeness or social faux pas, this designation implies a stable character disposition: one who consistently privileges personal needs and desires above communal norms and the legitimate interests of peers. Such individuals often employ manipulative tactics—ranging from passive-aggressive remarks to overt bullying—to secure their objectives, demonstrating little to no empathy for the emotional or psychological toll their behavior exacts. In academic parlance, they may be characterized by elevated scores on measures of antisocial personality traits, coupled with low agreeableness and a diminished capacity for perspective-taking.

From the vantage point of group dynamics and organizational behavior, assholes exert a disproportionate negative influence on climate and productivity. Their interactions are frequently marked by chronic disrespect, public humiliation of subordinates or colleagues, and an ingrained belief in personal superiority that dismisses feedback as irrelevant or flawed. This entrenched attitude corrodes trust, inhibits open communication, and precipitates stress or burnout among witnesses and victims.

Interventions aimed at mitigating such disruptive behavior typically involve clear boundary-setting, consistent enforcement of codes of conduct, and, when necessary, formal corrective action. In doing so, institutions affirm that while individual performance may be valued, it cannot come at the expense of collective psychological safety.

Bravo! ChatGPT. I couldn't say it better than that.

They're everywhere. On the road, in the drive-thru, behind you at the self-checkout machine in Walmart breathing like Darth Vader with an attitude problem. And every time one of them pops up in your life, it feels like a stress bomb detonates behind your eyes.

But here's the truth bomb you didn't know you needed: **Fu*k Them.**

Let that be your new traffic mantra. Let it be your emotional support phrase for aisle five when the woman with three screaming toddlers and a coupon binder the size of the Torah cuts in front of you with 83 items in the 20-items-or-less lane. Fu*k Them.

And I know what you're thinking: *"Reid, shouldn't I be more patient? More kind? Turn the other cheek?"*

No. You need to turn the wheel, the cart, or your energy *away*. Away from these chaos agents of daily life who wake up with a full tank of dumbass and a GPS set to "Other People's Boundaries."

Traffic: Your Car is Not a Confessional Booth

Let me start with a confession. I used to flip people off on the road. Not just a middle finger—I gave them the full Reid Mockery Symphony of Rage: horn honk, double bird, and a Broadway-worthy facial expression that said "I hope your latte spills and ruins your leather seats."

But you know what I learned? That energy—my energy—was being spent on people who would never remember me. They don't care that they nearly sideswiped me because they were watching a TikTok about cheese boards. They're already in their next moment of ignorance while I'm carrying their offense in my chest like a cracked rib.

So now I roll down the window, smile big like a southern debutante, and say, *"Fu*k you with grace."* Not out loud—just in my head. Then I turn up Beyoncé and move the hell on. That's the Fu*k Them way.

Restaurants: Where Common Sense Goes to Die

Ever had a server look you dead in the eyes and say, "We're out of that," *after* you've just waited 45 minutes and finally decided what to order? Yeah. Fu*k Them.

You could get mad. You could huff and puff and leave a two-star Yelp review titled *"WORST NIGHT OF MY LIFE"* even though it was just lukewarm soup. But here's what I want you to remember: It's a meal. Not a moral failure.

Let the restaurant screw up. Let the couple next to you argue about whether tip should be pre-tax or post-tax. Let the table of influencers film their drinks clinking thirty times. Fu*k Them. You're here to feed yourself, not solve the food service industry's shortcomings.

Ignorance: The World's Loudest Epidemic

Some people are just... committed to not learning. Ever. They will believe the dumbest Facebook headline from 2013 and fight you like it's the gospel.

Don't waste your breath. Seriously. If someone looks you in the face and says the earth is flat, and Walmart is a "private sovereign country," just nod slowly and think: *Fu*k Them.* Then walk away like you've got Taylor Swift's wind machine in your hair and nothing to prove.

I once had a family member tell me "college is for losers." I've got a Ph.D. in Problem People Studies, thank you very much. You think I argued? Nope. I grabbed a cheese stick, walked out of that conversation, and mentally added them to the **Fu*k Them Archives** under "Will Die on Wrong Hill."

And Then There's Walmart...

Let's be real: Walmart isn't just a store—it's a war zone of discount chaos. It's where boundaries go to die and entitlement breeds like mold in the produce aisle. You want to master the art of not giving a damn about assholes? Welcome to Walmart, baby. It's the training ground of the Fu*k Them mindset. And I've got three stories to prove it.

The Cart Commander

I'm in the deodorant aisle trying to make the deeply spiritual decision between "Arctic Ice" and "Unscented for Sensitive Pits," when a man with a Bluetooth earpiece (classic red flag) barrels his cart into mine like he's reenacting *Fast & Furious: Hygiene Drift.*

He doesn't say "sorry." He snorts. Then? He points at my cart and says, "You shouldn't block the whole aisle."

Oh. Really?

I could've explained that I wasn't blocking the aisle. I could've apologized to make it "less awkward." But Fu*k Them.

Instead, I smiled like a lunatic and said, "You're right. This is clearly your racetrack. Shall I pit stop into the Kotex aisle so you can take the turn?"

He muttered something about people being rude and stormed off to the protein powders.

Lesson? Assholes want a reaction. Let them stew in their own ego soup. Don't stir the pot—*turn off the stove.*

The Coupon Crusader

It's self-checkout. There's a woman ahead of me with a stack of coupons so thick you could use it to insulate a shed. Every beep of her coupon gets denied. Every denial is met with a screech for the manager, who is 19 years old and on the verge of tears.

People behind me are groaning. One guy fake coughs, "Get a life." And I almost—almost—say something.

But I remember: Fu*k Them. All of them.

The coupon lady? Maybe she's broke. Maybe she's lonely. Maybe coupons are the one thing she controls in her life.

So I pull out my phone, scroll TikTok, and let her fight her paper battle. Her war is not my war. Her chaos is not my circus.

You don't always have to step in, even when you're annoyed. Sometimes the strongest flex is non-engagement. Let them be dramatic. You? Be free.

The Parking Lot Prophet

Walmart parking lots are where humanity unravels. I park far away—on purpose—because I'm allergic to door dings and people who scream into phones while walking. As I'm loading groceries into my trunk, a man walks by, sees my "FU*K THEM" bumper sticker, and says:

"You must be real proud of that language."

I blink. Smile. Say, "I am."

He scoffs and walks off like he just exorcised my soul.

I could've explained myself. Could've defended the sticker. But here's the truth: I don't owe a stranger moral clarity in a Walmart parking lot.

The power move? Let them disapprove. Let them whisper. Let them clutch their pearls.

Because the more comfortable you are with disapproval, the freer you are to be yourself.

So yeah. Walmart isn't just a store. It's a stage. A test. A divine simulation of emotional resilience. And every time you choose peace over petty, stillness over shouting, boundaries over bullshit—you pass with honors.

Next time someone acts like a rotting onion in aisle six? Whisper it under your breath, Reid-style: Fu*k Them. Then grab your Arctic Ice, your peanut butter pretzels, and your dignity— and walk away like the confident badass you are.

If Target is a spa day, Walmart is a demolition derby inside a screaming toddler's fever dream.

You go in for shampoo and leave with a bruised soul and PTSD from watching a grown man yell at a cashier because the rotisserie chickens were "too moist." People treat the parking lot like a NASCAR pit lane. The aisles are war zones of abandoned carts, lost sandals, and someone live-streaming a conspiracy theory next to the cat litter.

So what do you do?

You *don't fight it*. You don't yell. You don't match their crazy. You let them cut in line. You let them scream. You let their toddler ride the motorized scooter into your shin. Fu*k Them.

Because if you let it, Walmart will eat your patience, your decency, and possibly your soul. You're not there to teach anyone manners. You're there to buy paper towels and get out with your sanity intact.

Here's the Truth:

You don't have to argue with every idiot. You don't have to explain yourself to every rude stranger. You don't have to fix the broken logic of internet trolls, restaurant Karens, or the man in the truck with six bumper stickers and a bullhorn.

You have one job: Protect your peace.

You do that by repeating these two words anytime an asshole crosses your path:

Fu*k Them.

Because they don't deserve your energy.

Because you don't have to absorb their chaos.

Because you're not here to be the emotional janitor of the world.

Now grab your receipt, get the hell out of Walmart, and go live your life like the calm, unbothered, glorious badass you are.

Fu*k Them. Always.

Animals can be assholes too.

It was the day I'd been waiting for my entire life. The meeting—the Big Zoom with a literary agent so high up the food chain her email signature had a *verified checkmark*. I'd spent weeks perfecting my pitch, rewriting my sample pages, and talking myself out of submitting a headshot from 2012 where I still had cheekbones.

I wore a blazer. Real pants. Lipstick. I even vacuumed the living room so my background screamed, "I'm put-together and emotionally stable!" Everything was ready.

Everything except Gus.

Now, Gus is my Boston Terrier. He's ten pounds of flat-faced chaos with a snort like a busted leaf blower. On a normal day, he spends 60% of his energy trying to lick outlets and the other 40% hunting down whatever food has fallen into a couch crevice. But that day? That day he had the eyes of a saboteur.

I clicked into the meeting. There she was—the agent. Polished. Smiling. Holding a mug that probably said something terrifying like "Query Slayer."

"Hi! It's so great to meet you," she said.

I was two sentences into my carefully memorized pitch when it happened.

Gus launched into frame like a possessed NFL wide receiver, a full-length string cheese flopping wildly from his mouth. He landed squarely behind me on the couch, looking directly into the camera like he had written the damn manuscript.

I froze. The agent blinked. Gus chomped.

"Oh! Is that a dog?" she asked, trying to be polite.

"Haha, yes, that's Gus," I said, praying he'd fall off the couch or spontaneously combust.

And then—of course—he vomited. On my shoulder. Mid-Zoom. A molten trail of cheese-laced horror that smelled like regret and moldy gym socks.

I made a strangled sound that definitely wasn't human. I saw the agent's face contort in that way people do when they're deciding whether to call animal control.

"I... think you have your hands full," she said, eyes wide. "Let's follow up later?"

Click.

Silence.

"Fu***KKK. Meeee!!!"**

Just me, Gus, and the hot mess of my literary dreams dissolving into a pile of Boston Terrier barf.

And Gus? He curled up at my feet, licked his butthole, and fell asleep like he didn't just destroy my entire future.

I haven't heard from the agent since. But that night, Gus got a bath and a bedtime story anyway—because despite being a monster with a nose that whistles when he breathes, he's my monster.

And one day... maybe he'll get the book deal.

Chapter Ten

Fu*k Them Emotions

Let's talk about emotional toddlers. Not the ones in diapers—those are adorable. I'm talking about grown-ass adults who throw tantrums like they're auditioning for a role on *The Real Housewives of Emotional Instability*. You know who I mean. The coworker who sulks for three days because their idea didn't get picked. The cousin who explodes at Thanksgiving because someone brought store-bought cranberry sauce. The boss who "feels disrespected" when you dare to ask a clarifying question. Yeah. Them.

Now, I need you to tattoo this on your frontal lobe: **Emotions last six seconds.** That's it. Six. Seconds. After that, the emotion becomes a *choice*. A decision. A performance. A manipulative little circus act that says, "Look at me, I'm the victim, the star, the misunderstood genius!" And if someone in your life keeps dragging their drama through the mud longer than it takes to microwave a burrito, I've got three words for you: **Fu*k. Them. Kindly.**

Emotional Immaturity: A Full-Time Job (Just Not Your Job)

Emotionally immature people are exhausting because they don't regulate, they escalate. They want you to *feel bad* for them, *fix* them, or *fear* them. It's a constant game of "Guess how I'm feeling, and cater to it, or I'll implode and blame you."

Listen—*you are not their emotional handler.* You are not the mood whisperer. And if they can't handle a six-second surge of discomfort without lashing out, icing people out, or guilt-tripping everyone in a 12-foot radius, they're not emotionally deep. They're emotionally *lazy*.

Want to know how to deal with them? You already do. It's in the title of this book: *Fu*k Them*.

Say it to yourself. Silently. With conviction. "Fu*k Them." Because you don't need to absorb their outbursts. You don't need to be the audience for their emotional puppetry.

Story Time: The Email Meltdown

A client once sent me an email in all caps. ALL. CAPS. Because I dared to suggest a change to the project *they* were paying me to do. The subject line? "I AM VERY DISAPPOINTED." (Yes, it was bolded. Yes, it was red.) This grown human being—CEO of a company, mind you—unleashed a six-paragraph rage rant over a font suggestion. Helvetica almost ended our business relationship.

Now, the old me? I'd over-apologize, stress for days, wonder if I was a terrible person. The new me? The one who discovered the Fu*k Them Theory?

I took a deep breath. I counted six seconds. I imagined her in a diaper with a juice box screaming about Comic Sans. And I whispered to myself, Fu*k her. I replied professionally. Not emotionally. Because she chose to be upset. I chose to not join her in the sandbox.

And guess what? Three days later, she apologized. Admitted she was overwhelmed and took it out on me. Why? Because I didn't feed the tantrum. I let her ride that emotional storm solo. I stayed grounded. Six seconds. That's all it took.

But What If It's Your Mom?

Here's where it gets tricky. What if the emotional toddler is someone you love? A parent, a partner, a best friend? I'm not saying cut them off. I'm saying set the thermostat. Don't let their storm freeze your day or overheat your peace.

When your mom guilt-trips you for not calling every day, say "Fu*k her" in your mind. Then call her when you have capacity. Not out of guilt. When your partner throws a mood fit because you dared to have boundaries, say "Fu*k them" (mentally) and stick to your boundary. Because people who love you don't weaponize their feelings against you. They don't make you feel like you're walking through a minefield made of eggshells.

You're not heartless. You're clear-headed. You're not cruel. You're calibrated.

And you're done being the emotional trash bin for every unprocessed feeling tossed your way.

Six Seconds, Baby

*The Fu*k Them Theory* isn't about being a jerk. It's about clarity. And science.

Here's what neuroscientists have discovered: an emotional trigger causes a chemical surge in the brain, and it lasts... six seconds. That's the time it takes for your brain to go "whoa," and your body to respond with heat, tightness, tears, rage—whatever. After that? The chemical reaction fades.

So if someone stays mad for six days?

They're not emotional.

They're indulgent.

They're not overwhelmed.

They're performing.

You, however, get to choose your role. Do you want to be cast in their one-woman show titled *Why I'm Always Right and Everyone Hurts Me?*

Or do you want to say, "Break a leg" and exit stage left with your sanity intact?

Final Note: Maturity is a Mirror

Being emotionally mature doesn't mean you *never* react. It means you choose when and how to respond. It means you give yourself six seconds. You let the feeling wash over you like a wave. And then? You act like a grown-up.

And when others don't?

You already know what to say.

Fu*k Them.

Silently. Gracefully. With peace in your heart and a boundary like a damn fortress. Because your life is not a daycare. And you're not in charge of anyone else's tantrums.

Fu*k Toxic Positivity – I'm Not Grateful, I'm Grieving

You ever been sad and someone chirps, *"Just be grateful"?* Yeah. *Fu*k Them.*

Let's talk about toxic positivity—that sugar-coated, sunshine-glazed gaslighting that turns real pain into a personal failure. Someone dies, and they say, *"Well, at least they're in a better place."* You lose your job, and they go, *"But now you can finally find your passion!"* You open up about depression and they hit you with, *"Thoughts become things!"*

Okay. Thoughts also become restraining orders. Keep talking.

Toxic positivity is emotional *bypassing*. It's what emotionally immature people do when they're too scared or uncomfortable to sit with the truth. They slap a glittery sticker on your wound and pretend it's healed.

Pain is not the problem. Pretending you're fine is.

The Lie of the Bright Side

There's this lie that if you just focus on the positive, the pain will disappear. But listen—if you put whipped cream on a turd, it's still a turd. Positive thinking doesn't fix everything. Sometimes you need to feel the thing, not fix it.

I've had days where I was drowning in grief, and some overly chipper person floated by in their inflatable optimism shouting, *"It's all happening for a reason!"* And I wanted to scream back, *"Yeah? What reason was THAT?!"*

Not everything happens for a reason. Sometimes, sh*t just happens. Period.

So what do you do when someone tries to glitter-bomb your grief?

You already know. Fu*k them.

Not loudly. Not angrily. Just internally. A little whispered rebellion. A refusal to perform gratitude for an audience that can't handle your humanity.

Story Time: When My Life Fell Apart and Karen Smiled

There was a month where everything fell apart. Marriage imploding. Finances trashed. I was living on microwaved sorrow and barely making rent. I told one of those hyper-positive acquaintances what was happening.

She said, *"Well, at least you still have your health!"*

My left eye twitched. My teeth clenched so hard I gave myself TMJ. I wanted to bite her. But instead, I took a breath. Six seconds. Let the emotional wave rise and fall. And I whispered—Fu*k her. Because she couldn't meet me in the dark. And that's not my burden.

Her comfort mattered more to her than my reality.

And that's when I realized: toxic positivity isn't kindness. It's cowardice dressed in cursive font.

Feel It or Repeat It

If you don't feel it, you repeat it. That's what toxic positivity skips. It says, "Don't cry, don't grieve, don't be angry—just think happy thoughts." And then those buried feelings rot in your gut like emotional leftovers no one ever throws out.

But here's the truth: **negative emotions are a gift.** They teach. They reveal. They're proof you're alive and paying attention. Anger means your boundary's been crossed. Sadness means something mattered. Guilt might mean growth is happening.

And yes, you can feel the hard things and still move forward. But only if you let yourself *feel* them first.

Your New Mantra: "I'm Not Okay—and That's Okay"

You don't have to smile when you're gutted. You don't have to be strong when you're shattered. You don't have to post a filtered selfie saying, "Living my best life" when your mascara's made of actual tears. You just have to be honest. And when someone tries to force sunshine down your throat when you're choking on sorrow?

You know what to do.

Six seconds. Deep breath. Whisper it in your mind like a protective spell:

Fu*k Them.

Then go feel what needs to be felt.

Because healing doesn't come from pretending.

It comes from permission.

Fu*k Codependency – You're Not a Life Raft, You're a Whole Damn Ship

Let's talk about those people who latch onto you like you're their personal emotional support animal. You know the type. If you don't respond to their text within 18 seconds, they think you hate them. If you have a boundary, they think you're "cold." If you say "no," they hear "abandonment."

Codependent people don't want a relationship. They want a host. A soft, spongy place to dump their chaos while you clean up the mess with a smile and a guilt hangover.

But here's the hard truth no one wants to say: that's not love. **That's dependence dressed up in a trauma costume.** And you don't have to audition for the role of Rescuer-in-Chief just because someone handed you a script.

You don't owe your peace to their panic.

You don't owe your energy to their dysfunction.

You sure as hell don't owe your soul to someone who only calls when their world is on fire—and somehow it's always on fire.

So what do we say?

Fu*k them. With love. From a distance. Behind a locked door.

Codependency Is Just Emotional Hunger in Drag

Let's get clear: being needed isn't the same as being loved. Codependent people confuse the two. They love how *you make them feel*—not who *you actually are.* You're not their partner. You're their life preserver.

And guess what happens if you stop floating?

They drown. And they blame you for it.

Healthy relationships have two whole people who can regulate their own emotions and respect each other's space. Codependent ones feel like an eternal group project where one person cries, and the other writes the essay, gives the speech, and gets zero credit.

Story Time: The Friend Who Always Needed "Just One More Thing"

I had a friend—we'll call her Shannon because her name was Shannon—who never called just to say hi. It was always a crisis. A breakup, a panic attack, a legal issue, a roommate fight. I was her unpaid therapist with a Ph.D. in Bullsh*t Management.

One night, I was in bed, burnt out, halfway through crying over a frozen pizza and *Yellowstone*, when she called me sobbing. "I need you," she said. "Right now. You're the only one who gets me."

And for a moment, I felt important.

Then I felt *trapped.*

That's what codependency does—it flatters and guilts you into staying on the hook. It makes you feel like their only hope, but also their only punching bag. Shannon didn't need me. She needed anyone to absorb her emotional wreckage.

And when I finally didn't answer? She said I abandoned her. No, Shannon. I chose myself.

But What If They're Family?

Oh, it gets spicier when it's blood. A parent who calls 12 times a day "just to check in." A sibling who can't make a single decision without a group text and a five-hour FaceTime. And if you don't answer? Suddenly you're "selfish."

Let me tell you something radical: *blood is not a hall pass for boundary violations.*

Say it again, slowly. Blood is not a hall pass.

You can love someone deeply and still say, *I am not your emotional outlet, your crisis concierge, or your surrogate nervous system.*

You can love someone and still whisper to yourself: Fu*k Them.

Then love them from a safe distance. With boundaries. With space. With the sacred power of no.

The Fu*k Them Theory Meets Codependency

Here's the truth that will set you free: you are not responsible for someone else's unhealed wounds. You didn't cause their trauma. You're not their savior. And you are absolutely allowed to say, *"That sounds hard. I hope you figure it out."*

That sentence alone might make a codependent person implode. Fu*k Them.

That's how they learn to self-soothe. That's how they learn to grow. And you? You get to reclaim your peace, your time, your life. You get to be whole, without stitching yourself to someone else's chaos. So next time someone emotionally grabs onto you like you're the last life raft on the Titanic?

Say it.

Breathe it.

Six seconds. Calm heart. Sharp mind.

Fu*k them.

And then float away on your own damn ship.

Fu*k the Guilt Trip – I'm Not Boarding That Flight

You know that heavy, sticky feeling in your chest when someone says, "Wow, I guess you don't care about me" just because you didn't drop everything to cater to their whims? That's not love. That's not respect. That's not connection.

That's manipulation with a sad trombone soundtrack.

It's called **guilt-tripping**, and it's the favorite airline of emotionally immature people. They book you on a nonstop flight to Shameville with a free carry-on of resentment and zero snacks. And guess what?

You don't have to get on that plane.

You can say no. You can feel peace. You can even smile while doing it. Because The Fu*k Them Theory doesn't just help you survive the guilt trip. It hands you the scissors to cut the damn ticket in half.

Guilt: The Great Emotional Mugging

Let's be honest—**guilt is one hell of a thief.** It robs your joy, your time, your energy, and worst of all, your *clarity*. It whispers that you're a bad daughter, a bad friend, a selfish jerk for not doing *more.*

And the worst part? Most of that guilt doesn't even come from you. It's manufactured. Guilt gets handed to you like a passive-aggressive casserole by people who want control disguised as "closeness."

Here's a brutal truth that'll set you free: if someone needs you to feel guilty in order to feel loved, their version of love is broken.

You are not bad for choosing rest.

You are not cruel for choosing distance.

You are not selfish for choosing you.

You're just no longer available for their emotional manipulation.

And that? That's growth, baby.

Story Time: The "Family Obligations" Scam

A few years ago, I skipped Christmas. Not out of spite. Not because I hate reindeer. I was burnt out. I needed solitude, sweatpants, and a weekend of nothing but silence and stuffing. I sent my regrets in advance. Polite. Honest.

My sister texted back: *"Wow. Guess we know where we rank."*

My aunt emailed: *"Your mother is so hurt. She was crying*

earlier."

Oh, and the kicker? My mom? Didn't actually care. She texted me a picture of her wine and said, *"Good call staying home."*

That guilt didn't come from love. It came from expectation. And when I didn't meet it, the peanut gallery started tossing shame grenades.

I almost folded. But instead?

Six seconds. Deep breath. Mental armor up.

Fu*k Them.

I spent Christmas curled up with a weighted blanket, a peppermint mocha, and *Elf*. It was perfect. And nobody died from my absence.

You don't owe your presence to people who weaponize it.

You don't owe your peace to someone else's performance of hurt.

You don't owe *anything* to anyone who thinks guilt is a form of currency.

But I Feel So Bad...

Of course you do. That's what makes you a good person. But being good doesn't mean being a doormat. You can care deeply and still not comply. You can love someone and still not leap every time they ring the shame bell.

When the guilt creeps in? Don't fight it. Just question it.

Ask yourself:

- *Is this guilt based in truth or obligation?*
- *Would I feel bad if they weren't disappointed?*
- *Am I betraying myself to make someone else feel better?*

And when the answer is, "Yeah, this guilt isn't mine," you know what to do.

Say it in your mind. Say it with power. Say it like a prayer for your peace:

Fu*k Them.
Then exhale.

Let the guilt fall off your shoulders like an old sweater that never fit right.

Final Thought: Guilt Isn't Love. Boundaries Are.

Love doesn't guilt you. It doesn't pressure, manipulate, or emotionally blackmail. Love says, "I see you. I respect your no. I want your *willing* yes."

Anything else?

It's control. And we don't do control around here. We do freedom. We do clarity. We do six-second resets, clear boundaries, and middle-finger energy *in our hearts*. So next time someone hands you a guilt trip with a smile?

Don't pack your bags. Don't explain yourself. Just mentally tear that ticket, walk away, and say—

Fu*k Them. I'm staying home.

Chapter Eleven

Your Looks: Fu*k Them

I remember the exact moment I realized I was living my life through the mirror. I was standing in my bathroom at seven a.m., trying on the same two outfits I'd cycled through for months—jeans that pinched at the waist and a top that hid every curve. My reflection looked back at me with tired eyes, silently judging that roll here, that dimple there. I felt hollow, drained, like I was shrinking into my own body instead of living in it. And in that moment, I heard my inner voice—scarier than any gym instructor or social-media troll—whisper: "You're not good enough. How do they even let people like you walk around?"

That voice wasn't mine; it was everyone else's. Family members commenting on my "need to lose weight." Exes reminding me, politely or not, that I could be "so much prettier." Random strangers in coffee shops thinking it's their business to lecture me on self-control. The meme culture that glorified thigh gaps and waist trainers. The fitness gurus shaming anyone who dared to enjoy a donut. It was a chorus of outside noise, and I let it drown out my own voice for far too long.

But let me tell you something I wish I'd known back then: none of that matters. Your body, your face, your "imperfections"—Fu*k Them!

The Culture of Self-Hatred

We live in a world that equates attractiveness with worth. How often have you seen an ad promising "Instant confidence! Lose 10 pounds in 10 days!"? Or 20 influencers waxing poetic about "self-love" while secretly pushing detox teas and airbrushing their photos? It's a setup. A trap. They create the problem—your perceived flaws—and then peddle the solution, pretending it's a path to self-esteem. But here's the brutal truth: no product or Photoshop filter can give you genuine confidence. Confidence has to come from you. Not from anyone else telling you that you're acceptable only if you fit their narrow definition of beauty.

I spent years pinning inspirational quotes about self-love on my vision board while simultaneously stepping on the scale every morning. I was a walking contradiction—reading books about body positivity while returning workout clothes I couldn't bring myself to slip into. I thought I was too smart to fall for marketing gimmicks, but I was actually a perfect target. Why? Because I believed the underlying lie: my body dictated my value.

Let me break down how the cycle usually goes:

1. **Comparison:** You scroll through Instagram and see someone who "has it all" — slender, flawless, living their best life.
2. **Self-Judgment:** You start measuring yourself up, thinking, "If only I looked like that, my life would be better."
3. **Chasing Perfection**: You sign up for a diet plan, buy expensive workout gear, torture yourself with exhausting routines—hoping that if you do X, Y, and Z, finally you'll be "enough."
4. **Failure and Shame:** Inevitably, you slip. You skip a workout. You binge on pizza. You feel like a failure, and that shame fuels more dieting, more self-loathing.

Rinse and repeat—until one day you wake up, missing precious moments with friends and family because you're "too busy" fixing a problem that doesn't really exist.

We've all been there. And that's exactly why it's time to flip the script.

My Wake-Up Call

I was thirty-one when I finally said "Fu*k this" to the entire ordeal. I was in my car, parked outside my high school reunion venue. My phone buzzed with the usual group chat notifications: who was wearing what, who had "really let themselves go," who was "looking fabulous." My chest tightened as I scrolled through the photos of my classmates—everyone seemingly fit, polished, traveling the world. Meanwhile, I was in yoga pants with a suspicious coffee stain, eating a protein bar that tasted like chalk. My palms sweated. My heart thumped. I felt like I was about to crawl under the seat and disappear.

And then my best friend called me. She said, "Hey, I see you drove into the parking lot. Seriously, please don't bail. I've been looking forward to this for weeks." I glanced at my reflection in the rearview mirror. I saw the tiredness, the insecurity. I almost turned the key, about to drive home, cancel my flight, hide. But then I thought: Why am I letting a room full of people I haven't talked to since graduation dictate my self-worth?

I took a deep breath, grabbed my purse, and walked in. Yes, I felt judged. Yes, there were whispers. But here's what happened next: As soon as I stepped into the crowd, my friend hugged me so tightly that I couldn't focus on anyone else's judgment. We laughed, we caught up, and I realized that 90% of the people there were too busy worrying about their own "imperfections" to waste energy on mine. Because guess what? Everyone is busy managing their own insecurities.

That night I made a vow: I am not defined by my body. I am not a before-and-after photo pinned to the fridge. I will never let someone else's standards override my own happiness. And you know what? It felt revolutionary.

The Anatomy of "Fu*k Them" for Your Looks

So, how do you get from "Oh my god, I look terrible" to "Your looks? Fu*k them"? It's not a magic pill. It's a process. Here's the breakdown:

1.   **Identify the Voices:** Start by writing down every critical thought you've ever heard about your body—parents, ex-partners, social media ads, random strangers. Seeing them on paper helps you realize these are external, not internal. They aren't you.

2.   **Define Your Priorities:** What truly matters in your life? Is it scrolling through Instagram comparing yourself? Or is it waking up and doing things that bring you joy—writing, dancing, building relationships? Make a list of your top five life priorities. Spoiler: "Obeying societal beauty standards" won't make the cut.

3.   **Daily "Fu*k Them" Exercise:** Set aside five minutes each morning. Look in the mirror and say, out loud if you can: "Your opinion of my body is none of my business." (Yes, some people will stare as you do this. Good! They're not as confident as you.)

Follow up with one genuine compliment to yourself: "I handled that project at work like a boss. My body doesn't define that."

Do this for 30 days. Consistency rewires your brain.

4. **Detox from Comparison Triggers:** Unfollow social accounts that make you feel bad. If your aunt keeps sending you weight-loss meal plans, block her texts for a while. Remove apps that turn you into a judge instead of a human being.

5. **Celebrate What Your Body Does, Not Just How It Looks:** Can you laugh so hard your belly jiggles? Can you hug someone tight? Can you walk, dance, breathe? That's powerful. Make a list of five things your body has done for you this month—big or small—and revisit it whenever you need a reminder.

6. **Redefine "Self-Care":** Self-care is not just bubble baths and face masks. It's also setting boundaries with people who comment on your weight. It's saying "no" to that dinner invitation if all you'll do is feel judged. It's treating your body as a vessel for living fully, not a project to be "fixed." Definitely watch "Parks and Recreation" Season 4, Episode 4, titled "Pawnee Rangers." Treat Yo Self!

Remember: every time you think, "I wish I looked like X," you're giving someone else power over your happiness. And who gives a flying Fu*k about their standards? The sooner you stop playing by rules you didn't write, the faster you'll reclaim your life.

Real Talk—It's Not Always Easy

Alright, listen. I'm not going to sugarcoat it: when you first start telling people to "Fu*k Them" about your looks, there will be backlash. People might say, "If you just tried harder," or "You'd be prettier if…" You'll hear the unsolicited advice, the side-eye at family gatherings, maybe even a "We love you, but..." It's crappy. Here's how to handle it:

- **Prepare a Script:** When Aunt Karen cornered you at Thanksgiving last year, I had this ready: "Aunt Karen, I appreciate that you care, but my body isn't up for debate. Let's talk about something else."

- **Use Humor as Armor:** If someone says, "Don't you think you should..." you reply, "Nah, I'm busy living my best life—why don't you take notes?" A little sarcasm can shut down the conversation fast.

- **Surround Yourself with Allies:** Find friends, join online communities, read blogs by women and men who've reclaimed their bodies. You need a support system that celebrates your journey.

- **Give Yourself Grace:** Some days, you'll slip back into old habits—dieting, comparing. That's normal. When you catch yourself, don't beat yourself up. Just say, "Hey, thanks for showing up. But I'm moving on." Then pivot: go do something you love.

Stories of "Fu*k Them" Triumphs

- *The Wedding Dress Revelation:* One friend, Susan, spent three months starving herself for her wedding. On the day she tried on dresses? She looked in the mirror, burst into tears, and said, "I refuse to let a number define how I get married." She picked a dress two sizes larger, danced in it, and had the best day of her life. Six months later, she's still living unapologetically, and the photos show the happiest bride you'll ever see. Fu*k Them.

- *The Boardroom Breaking Point:* I had a colleague who was passed over for a promotion, not because she wasn't talented, but because some executives commented on her "lack of polish" and "too many curves." The day she found out, she stormed into their office and said, "If my body disqualifies me, then your company doesn't deserve me." She walked out and started her own consultancy. Today, she's thrice as successful—and she has no office dress code except "Be you." Fu*k Them.

- *The Social Media Detox:* Another friend, Jess, was addicted to filters and face-tune apps. She'd post a photo and immediately scrutinize it, reading every comment for praise or criticism. One morning, she deleted her entire Instagram. She spent that weekend hiking with her partner, feeling the sun on her actual skin. She returned to social media a month later with a new handle: @FlawsAndAll. She now posts unedited photos— freckles, wrinkles, and all—and has become an inspiration to thousands. Fu*k Them.

Your Homework

I wouldn't be Mel Robbins (or Reid Mockery, if we're being real) without giving you an action step. So here it is:

1. **Mirror Talk**: Tomorrow morning, stand naked or wearing whatever you'd normally feel insecure in. Look yourself in the eyes and say: "Your looks, Fu*k them." Then list three things you love about what your body DOES—not how it looks. Maybe it's your scars, your laugh lines, the fact that you can hug someone so tight they can't breathe. Write those down.

2. **Letter to Your Younger Self:** Write a letter to the person you were when you first started doubting your body. Be brutally honest. Tell them what you know now: that they were worthy of love and respect regardless of appearance. Let that

letter live on your desk or in your phone. Read it whenever doubt creeps in.

3.   **Set a Boundary:** Identify one person or situation that triggers body shame. That might be a family dinner with commentary-laden food, or binge-scrolling an Instagram account that makes you feel like crap. Decide right now: will you set a boundary, mute, unfollow, or calmly tell them to stfu? Put it in writing and actually do it this week.

The Fat Shots

I know some people are having success with this, but I don't trust it yet.

I am not here to burst your Ozempic bubble: this isn't a magic wand, it's a chemical drill. Sure, you'll gobble less because nausea, vomiting, and stomach spasms become your new BFFs, but don't pretend that's a winning trade. Your pancreas might stage a revolt (hello, pancreatitis), your gallbladder could demand eviction (gallstones, anyone?), and if you ignore the warning signs, you'll find yourself in a hospital bed faster than you can say "weight-loss journey." Animal studies even hint at thyroid tumors (okay, mostly in rats, but still—do you really want to bet on your neck staying intact?), and if your blood sugar tanks, you could be trading salad for an ambulance. Did I mention the weekly injections aren't free? Your wallet takes a bigger hit than that extra slice of cheesecake you thought you'd avoid.

And let's not forget the mental gymnastics: one minute you're high-fiving yourself for dropping pounds, the next you're spiraling into "am I ever thin enough?" anxiety. Quit Ozempic and watch your appetite stage a comeback tour, complete with rebound weight gain and mood swings that rival a Kardashian tweetstorm. Plus, that rapid weight loss? Say hello to a saggy epidermis no Spanx can fix. And look up Ozempic Feet. Talk about heebie jeebies?

Bottom line: if you're desperate enough to try this, okay— just don't clutch that syringe like it's the Holy Grail. Do your homework, talk to a real doctor, and remember: your health, your choice. If anyone gives you shit for being cautious, look 'em dead in the eye and say, "Fuck them—my life, my rules."

Closing Mantra

Let me close with this: You are not your body. You are a force of nature. Every wrinkle, stretch mark, scar, and curve is a battle scar, a memory, a testament to your resilience. If the world tries to tell you otherwise—Fu*k them. They built their standards on filters, on ancient prejudices, on unattainable ideals. You? You build your standards on authenticity, on joy, on the audacity to be fully yourself.

So tomorrow, when you wake up and that old voice tries to tell you "not good enough," shut it down with: "Your looks, Fu*k them." Because in the end, the only opinion that matters is yours. The only mirror you owe an explanation to is the one inside your soul—and trust me, it's a hell of a lot kinder than any stranger's comment.

Now go out there and live like you mean it. Fu*k their standards. Embrace your power. And remember: every time you say "Fu*k them" to the haters, you're one step closer to freedom.

Chapter Twelve

Fu*k Them
Mark Manson Fans

*Stop Giving a Fu*k vs. Start Saying Fu*k Them: A Brutally Honest Comparison of Mark Manson and Reid Mockery's Self-Help Smackdowns*

Let's be clear from the start: both Mark Manson's *The Subtle Art of Not Giving a Fu*k* and Reid Mockery's *The Fu*k Them Theory* are not here to make you feel better. They're here to slap your face with the truth—and maybe a touch of sarcasm. But that's about where the similarities end.

Tone and Delivery:

Mark Manson:
Cynical. Slick. Rational. Mark is like the friend who sips black coffee, tells you your ex was emotionally stunted, and backs it up with a Nietzsche quote. His book is structured like a TED Talk in combat boots—clean, tough, with a little philosophical fluff.

Reid Mockery:
Reid is your vodka aunt with a PhD in "Problem People Studies." She doesn't sip—she gulps, then tells you to stop making PowerPoints about your boundaries and just say Fu*k you out loud. She's raw, vulgar, and hilarious in the same sentence. If Mark is your logical brain, Reid is your middle finger.

Message Focus:

Manson's Core Message:
Stop caring about everything. You have a limited number of f*cks to give, so spend them wisely. Suffering is inevitable. Accept it. Choose better problems.

Mockery's Core Message:
You're not the problem—*they are.* Stop bending your life around assholes. If someone doesn't like your boundaries, your vibe, your dog sweater, or your opinions on Hamilton? Fu*k Them. You're not here to manage their discomfort.

Audience Energy:

Manson Fans:
People who want enlightenment but aren't ready to fully cut ties with their therapists. They highlight passages. They journal. They love the phrase "emotional bandwidth."

Mockery Fans:
People who've had enough. The recently fired, dumped, betrayed, or just existentially done. They don't want peace—they want *power.* They underline sentences with a knife. They read Reid with one hand and flip someone off with the other.

Structure:

Manson:
Chapters are like philosophical essays with punchlines. He walks you through his logic, then slaps you with a conclusion.

Mockery:
Reid writes like she's yelling across a Walmart parking lot

after catching her cousin in a Karen moment. Her chapters are structured chaos: stories, rants, fake studies, sidebars about her Boston Terrier, and a brutal clarity that makes you laugh and finally send that "Do not contact me again" text.

Best One-Liner Showdown:

Manson: "Who you are is defined by what you're willing to struggle for."

Mockery: "If Karen's offended by your silence, imagine what a full fu*k-off would do."

Final Thoughts:

Mark Manson helps you manage your existential dread.
Reid Mockery helps you weaponize it.
Manson is the breakup text.
Mockery is the flaming bag of dog poop on the doorstep.
Manson teaches you to let go.
Mockery reminds you to *let go of them first*—then slam the damn door.
In the end, both books are needed. One gives you a new mindset. The other gives you a megaphone. So the choice is yours:
Do you want to *stop giving a Fu*k?*
Or do you want to *start saying Fu*k Them?*

Chapter Twleve

Take Away from the Fu*k Them Theory

I understand that some parts of this may feel repetitive, but I want to emphasize that this is a parody. I challenge you to count how many times Mel Robbins repeats herself throughout the book. While I believe you grasped the key points within the first ten pages, some people need reminders about these concepts.

You know what doesn't work?

Contorting yourself into emotional origami just to please people who wouldn't water you if you were on fire.

That's where *The Fu*k Them Theory* steps in like a well-dressed bouncer at the club of your peace of mind. It works not because it's trendy. Not because it's catchy. It works because it gives you permission to stop performing for the emotionally constipated masses and finally take care of your own damn nervous system.

So, Why Does It Work?

1. It Stops the Emotional Hijacking.

You get cut off in traffic. Your mom sends another passive-aggressive Bible verse. Becky from accounting double books your meeting *again*. Before this theory, you'd stew, spiral, and strategize the perfect clapback.

Now? You silently say, **Fu*k Them.**

Boom.

Your brain doesn't go DEFCON 1. Your stress hormone cortisol doesn't flood your body like emotional sewage. Your blood pressure? Normal. Your dignity? Intact.

2. It Pulls the Plug on People-Pleasing.

We've been groomed—especially women—to bend, mold, and shrink. *The Fu*k Them Theory* isn't about *being* rude. It's about reclaiming your space without a permission slip. You don't need to justify your boundaries. Just say, in your head (not always out loud unless you like HR meetings),

Fu*k Them.

3. It Restores Your Focus.

You were never supposed to carry everyone else's emotional garbage like some overworked feelings janitor. The Fu*k Them Theory lets you drop their drama on the curb, where it belongs, so you can focus on your *own* to-do list, dreams, and dog's gastrointestinal issues. (Gus, I'm looking at you.)

4. It Keeps You Silent but Powerful.

This theory isn't about going nuclear. It's about going *neutral.* It's internal. Mental. Like a cussword-flavored meditation. It's the opposite of revenge. It's release. You're not bottling it up—you're letting it float away on a raft made of mental middle fingers.

5. It Doesn't Require Them to Change.

That's the kicker. This isn't "Fix Them Therapy." They can stay messy, loud, opinionated, unreliable, manipulative, or just plain dumb. Fu*k Them *isn't for them.* It's for you. You take back control by letting go of the illusion that they ever owed you decency in the first place.

The Bridge to Fu*k Me

But here's the turn you didn't see coming.

If all you ever say is Fu*k Them, *you stay stuck in reaction mode. You're still giving them the wheel—just yanking it in the other direction.*

That's where Fu*k Me comes in.

Fu*k Me is *ownership.*

It's when you stop just dodging bullets and start disarming the whole damn gun.

Fu*k Me means:

- Maybe I did overextend myself to be liked.
- Maybe I ignored red flags and called them confetti.
- Maybe I kept expecting someone to act differently than they always have.
- Maybe I gave too many chances to people who only give me migraines.

Fu*k Me isn't shame. It's *accountability with a smirk.*

It's not "I'm the problem." It's "I'm in control."

You're not just burning bridges—you're building boundaries.

You're not bitter. You're **brilliantly unavailable to non-sense.**

The Benefits of the Full Theory—Fu*k Them to Fu*k Me

1. Emotional Regulation: You stop spiraling over every idiot in your orbit.

2. Mental Clarity: You learn what's yours and what's not.

3. Inner Peace: You don't chase closure. You say, "No thank you," and close the damn door.

4. Boundaries with Bite: You stop bleeding energy on people who wouldn't even give you a Band-Aid.

5. Growth: You stop blaming and start building. You shift from defense to offense—*your life becomes yours again.*

It's not just a theory.
It's not just a phrase.
It's your freakin' power cord.

Fu*k Them is the detox.
Fu*k Me is the upgrade.

So plug in, sis.
We've got sh*t to do.

Look. If you've made it to the end of this book, you're either:

A) Nodding like a maniac because someone *finally* said what you've been thinking for years, or

B) Clutching your pearls and trying to decide whether to send me hate mail or a fruit basket.

Either way, I win.

*The Fu*k Them Theory* isn't about rage. No. This theory is a stress strategy. A silent rebellion. A deep, soul-cleansing mental shrug that says, "I am no longer setting myself on fire to keep your insecure ass warm."

Because guess what? You don't owe anyone your peace. And you sure as hell don't need to invite other people's emotional clutter into your already cluttered brain just because you feel guilty or polite. Guilt is not a growth strategy. Neither is being everyone's unpaid therapist, punching bag, or PR agent.

The truth? People will disappoint you. They'll talk shit. They'll demand apologies for how your boundaries make them uncomfortable. Let them. Then mentally—and silently—say it with me:

Fu*k. Them.

It's your internal exhale. Your mini-meditation. It's like yoga, but without the camel pose or pants that give you a yeast infection. Just eight letters. One thought. Instant clarity.

When you stop trying to fix people who don't want fixing...

When you stop justifying your joy to people who prefer you miserable...

When you stop apologizing for who you are, what you think, and what you've overcome...

That's when *you* take the power back.

So here's your homework:

1. Say "Fu*k Them" (silently, for legal reasons) next time someone tries to guilt you.

2. Say it when someone sends a 3-paragraph text about why they're mad you didn't come to their MLM party.

3. Say it when your boss expects 9 p.m. emails and your bladder's still full from lunch.

4. Say it when your ex posts a humblebrag.

5. Say it when someone tries to steal your peace—and your last fry.

Because your peace? That sh*t's priceless.

Oh, and before I forget: Get the Hardback Version of this book.

Why?

Because it's heavy enough to knock some sense into your cousin who keeps dating men named "Kylee" with three E's.

Because it makes a perfect passive-aggressive gift for your office Secret Santa.

Because when people see a hardback with giant letters that say Fu*k Them, they'll know you've entered your villain era—and they'll back the hell off.

You've got the theory. Now go live it.

Boldly. Bravely. And with a sparkle in your eye that says, "I don't have time for this emotional tap dance anymore."

This is not goodbye.

This is just:

Fu*k Them. Forever.

With love (and zero apologies),

Reid Mockery, Ph.D.

Your certified expert in Problem People Studies

(And proud owner of one emotionally unavailable Boston Terrier)

Your Assignment

Dear Badass Readers,

First off, thank you. Thank you for picking up *The Fu*k Them Theory,* for turning its pages, and for embracing its bold message. When I decided to drop an F-bomb in the title of my book, I knew it was a gutsy move – but you got it. You understood exactly why I did it, and you didn't shy away. I am beyond grateful for your support, your open minds, and your willingness to join me on this unapologetic journey.

Writing this book was my way of saying enough to all the people-pleasing and approval-chasing that hold us back. Seeing you read it, share it with friends, and live out its message means the world to me. You've proven that there are so many of us ready to stop giving a damn about the naysayers and start living life on our own terms. Your enthusiasm – the late-night messages, the social media shout-outs, and the conversations I've seen you spark – has blown me away. I couldn't be prouder to have readers like you who are unafraid to stand up and say, "Yes, I'm doing me – if someone doesn't like it, f**k them!"

This whole idea was sparked by Mel Robbins and her original *The "Let Them" Theory.* Mel's two simple words – "Let them" – have helped millions break free from worrying about other people's opinion. Her work ignited a spark within me. I thought, hell, let's crank that idea up a notch! So Mel, if you're reading this: thank you for lighting the spark. Your groundbreaking mindset gave me the courage to add my own twist and voice.

Now, dear reader, I have a small favor to ask – actually, a few favors. If my book has made you laugh, inspired you, pissed you off in a good way, or given you that jolt of confidence to live louder, I want to hear about it. More importantly, others need to hear about it. Your voice is powerful, and it can help spread this message and grow our community of bold, fearless individuals.

Here's how you can make a difference.
• Leave a written review. Post a quick review on Amazon, Goodreads, or wherever you bought *The Fu*k Them Theory.* Your honest thoughts – what you loved, what challenged you – help other people discover the book. Plus, I read every review. Seriously, every single one. Your feedback not only fuels me, it helps others decide to join our movement.

• Post a video review or reaction. If you're feeling extra fired up, grab your phone and film yourself talking about the book. Whether it's a 60-second TikTok, an Instagram Reel, or a longer YouTube review, let it rip. Be real, be raw, be you. Did a particular chapter make you yell "hell yes!" or change how you handle haters? Tell that story on camera. I can't tell you how amazing it is to see your faces and hear your voices sharing the Fu*k Them attitude in living color.

• Share your story on social media. Spread the word on Facebook, Instagram, TikTok – wherever you hang out. Drop your favorite quote or the biggest lesson you took away from the book. I love seeing our message out in the wild, and I often share reader posts. Your story might be exactly what someone else needs to hear to feel empowered.

Why am I asking for all this? Because your voice matters. This isn't just my book; it's our book, our movement. Every review you write and every story you share lights the way for someone else. When a potential reader sees your review or your social post, they're not just hearing from some author with a crazy title – they're hearing from a real person who's living it. You are the proof that the Fu*k Them mindset works. You're showing the world what it looks like to live boldly and not apologize for it.

So once again, from the bottom of my heart: thank you. Thank you for reading, for caring, for daring to live life on your terms. Thank you for every time you've said "f**k them" to the doubters or toxic influences in your world. And thank you for being part of this journey with me.

Also by Reid Mockery

Fourth Wing Parody: Fifth Wing
Iron Flame Parody: Purple Flame
The Housemaid Parody: The Horsemaid
*Where The Crawdads Sh*t*
Divergent Parody: Detergent
Fifty Shades of Beige Trilogy
The Fault is All Yours

Bibliography

Compiled by Reid Mockery, Ph.D. — because even bullsh*t needs footnotes.*

Books and Monographs

• Blartman, S. & Wince, D. (2003). *Emotional Vampires and the People Who Feed Them: A Guide to Draining the Drama.* University of Passive-Aggressive Press.

• Dickerman, F. (2011). *The Subtle Art of Not Giving a Single Sh*t Until It's Too Late.* Misfit Publishing Group.

• Snark, I. M. (1999). *Burn Bridges Like You Built Them Yourself: A Pyromaniac's Guide to Boundaries.* Smoke Signal Press.

• Fucher, L. A. (2022). N*o is a Full Fu*cking Sentence: How to End Conversations with Eye Contact and Caffeine Breath.* Bold Type Books.

• Mockery, R. (2024). *Profanity Pilates: Stretching Your Patience While Flipping the Bird.* Uppercut Wellness Series, Vol. 2.

Academic Journals and Research Papers

• Glitt, B. & Moore, C. (2017). *"Cognitive Responses to Middle Finger Gestures in High-Stress Scenarios."* Journal of Unverified Neuroscience, 11(4), 69–420.

• Chong, T. & Valdez, K. (2020). *"The Impact of Saying 'Fu*k Them' Silently During Thanksgiving Dinner: A Longitudinal Family Study."* Intergenerational Trauma & Turkey Quarterly, 34(2), 112–118.

• Painson, D. (2016). *"Emotional Detachment in the Age of Group Texts: A Meta-Analysis of Ghosting as Self-Care."* Journal of Digital Dysfunction, 19(3), 404–Not Found.

- Wu, B. (2021). *"Swear Words as Stress Regulators: A Randomized Controlled Trial in a Florida Walmart."* Psychological Irregularities Monthly, 7(9), 1776–1779.
- Trollen, B., & Skorn, H. (2015). *"Boundary Setting in the Workplace: A Study of Strategic Chair-Spinning and Passive Aggressive Snack Labeling."* Corporate Avoidance Review, 3(2), 8–47.

Conference Proceedings and Unpublished Papers

- Mockery, R. (2023). *Fu*k Them to Their Faces: Vocalization as Liberation.* Presented at the 1st Annual Summit of Weaponized Wellness, hosted by the University of Nowhere.
- Elbows, R. (2019). *"Biting Your Tongue and Developing Lockjaw: Consequences of Not Cussing Out Carol from HR."* Abstract accepted but banned at the International Symposium of Unspoken Rage.
- Pluntz, Y. (2018). *Anger, Guilt, and the Great Ghosting Migration of 2018: A Case Study in Digital Disappearances.* Basement Press.

Other Sources

- Anonymous (2020). Reddit Thread: *AITA for Telling My Cousin to Go Fu*k Himself?* Retrieved from /r/BoundariesAreBeautiful.
- @QueenOfNope (2023). *"If you're offended, that's a you problem. Blocked."* [Tweet]. X, formerly Twitter, formerly a mental health minefield.
- DMs from Chad (n.d.). Screenshots archived under "Evidence.txt."
- Voice Memo, Mom, 4:22 AM (2022). "You're just like your father, but worse." Replayed 89 times for emotional clarity.

Printed in Dunstable, United Kingdom